AVKO Sequential Spelling 2

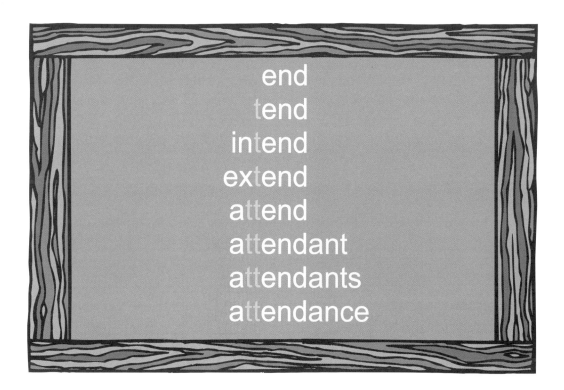

end
tend
intend
extend
attend
attendant
attendants
attendance

by

Don McCabe
Research Director
AVKO Educational Research Foundation

Dedication

This book is dedicated to:
All the members of the AVKO Educational Research Foundation
and especially to the memory of one of its first members,

Mary Clair Scott
without whose work and devotion to the cause of literacy,
the AVKO Foundation might never have gotten off the ground,

Betty June Szilagyi
who was my first and by far my most important teacher,

Devorah Wolf
without whose encouragement and commitment
to the ideals of AVKO
this edition would not be possible,

Ann, Robert, and Linda McCabe
all of whom have sacrificed much of their time and energy
helping AVKO grow
as well as all those friends and relatives
who have been a source of encouragement.

May this book help you to help others improve their abilities to read and write.

1 2 3 4 5 6 7 8 9 10 11 Printing   Year 03 93 92 89 87 85 83 81 79 76 74

Publisher's Cataloging in Publication Data
McCabe, Donald J.
          1. Spelling—Miscellanea 2. Reading—Miscellanea 3. Curriculum—Miscellanea 4. Literacy.
Library of Congress Subject Headings: Spelling, Reading, Curriculum
Library of Congress Classification Number: LB1050.2F79
Library of Congress Card Number: To be determined
Dewey Decimal Classification Number 428.4
ISBN: 1-56400-962-9

AVKO Educational Research Foundation, Inc.
3084 Willard Road
Birch Run, MI 48415
Telephone: (810) 686-9283 FAX (810) 686-1101
Websites: www.avko.org and www.spelling.org Email: info@avko.org

The Basic Concepts of Teaching Spelling by Word Families

You may have used the concept of rhyming words that have the same letter endings to help your students learn to read. For example, you may have introduced the word *at*, then also shared *cat*, *bat*, *sat*, and maybe even *scat*. Unfortunately, you have never had any source book for finding all the rhyming words with the same spelling patterns. [NOTE: In the latest academic jargon word families are now called "rimes." The consonants, consonant blends, and digraphs that precede the word family (or rime) are now called onsets. Use whatever term you wish with your students. In this book, I generally use the terms *base* or *word family* rather than the new jargon word "rime."]

The Patterns of English Spelling (formerly *Word Families Plus*) is now available to be used as a source book so that you can teach any word family. This is not just a simple collection of word lists. This book consists of complete patterns to help your students (and quite often parents and teachers!) see patterns that exist and to lock in on those patterns with their "computer" brains. For example, I believe that if you can teach your students (or anyone) the word *at*, you can also teach them:

bat	bats	batted	batting		
cat	cats				
scat	scats				
flat	flats	flatted	flatting		
pat	pats	patted	patting		
spat	spats				
mat	mats	matted	matting		
rat	rats	ratted	ratting		
batter	batters	battered	battering	battery	batteries
flatter	flatters	flattered	flattering	flattery	
matter	matters	mattered	mattering		
battle	battles	battled	battling		
cattle					
rattle	rattles	rattled	rattling		

OR, for a more sophisticated example, from the word **act** you can build:

act	acts	acted	acting	active	action
fact	facts				
tract	tracts				traction
attract	attracts	attracted	attracting	attractive	attraction
distract	distracts	distracted	distracting		distraction
extract	extracts	extracted	extracting	extractive	extraction
subtract	subtracts	subtracted	subtracting		subtraction
contract	contracts	contracted	contracting		contraction

Perhaps the most important difference between the traditional approach to spelling and the AVKO (**A**udio-**V**isual-**K**inesthetic-**O**ral) approach is that we use tests as a **learning** device and **not** as a method of **evaluation**. I believe that the natural method of learning is learning from mistakes, and that is why I want children to correct their own mistakes **when** they make them—so they can learn from them.

We developed the *AVKO Sequential Spelling Tests* to utilize the word family approach sequentially and to apply the very simple techniques of having students correct their own mistakes **when** they make them—not hours, days, or even weeks later.

Use a Dry Erase Board or Something Similar to Give AVKO Sequential Spelling Tests

---

The First Day

On your first day of using Sequential Spelling 2, share with your students:

I have some good news and some bad news. First the bad news. Today and every day until we finish this book, we are going to have a spelling test. The good news is that each one of you will correct your own paper. But before we start, I want each of you to take out a sheet of paper and put your name on it. Did you spell your name correctly? Good. That's my first test. My next test is like a doctor's test. It's not for a grade so don't worry about it. Okay? Now write the following sentence:

My brother has a nephew who is older than he is.

If any of your students shows signs of struggling with the sentence, just ask them to try to spell the word **nephew** only. If they still find it difficult to put down anything, ask them to just put down—in any order—some of the letters that might be in the word *beginning.*

Now collect their papers.

On the 5th day, you will be able to demonstrate that your students who couldn't spell **nephew** on the first day were able to correctly spell it without ever having seen or studied the word. And remember that according to Harry Greene's *The New Iowa Spelling Scale* (1954) only 1% of all public school 3rd graders can be expected to spell this word and just barely 63% of all public school 8th graders can spell the word **nephew**! We will expect that you will point that out to your students on the 5th day.

If your students have their own copy of the *AVKO Student Response Book for Sequential Spelling*, have them open their books to page 3. Note the location of Day 1. It is in the *middle* column of page 3. Day 2 is in the middle column on page 5. Day 3 is in the middle column on page 7. Day 4 is in the middle column on page 9, and so forth. Please note the AVKO motto on the bottom of these pages:

Mistakes are Opportunities to Learn

The reason for this arrangement is to prevent children from copying the base word that they had the day before and then just adding the -s, -ed, or -ing ending as the case may be. Just as children don't learn by copying from others, they don't learn by copying from themselves.

If you do not use the student response books, you can have your students take out a clean sheet of paper. Use a clean sheet for every day.

● *In the column marked 1st day/Lesson 1, please write the word "**chew**" as in: "You're not supposed to **chew** gum in here. **chew**. If you don't get it right, it's no big deal! You may erase it and write it correctly.*

After your students have attempted writing **chew**, ask them what the first two letters of **chew** are. Hopefully they will shout out, "CH!" Now, you write on the dry erase board (or something similar) just the letters "ch." Now ask what the last two letters of **chew** are. Again, they might shout out, "EW!" If anyone shouts out O or OO or OU or U, tell them those were good guesses, but ...

On the dry erase board you now show the -ew. (It really doesn't matter what color you use for the E and the W. I personally like to use green for the word family patterns to contrast later on with the black *beginning letters.*)

Depending upon the age of your students and their attitudes, you may try to get them to spell aloud the word with you (the oral channel) as they trace over their corrected spelling (the kinesthetic channel).

● Then give the second word, **crew** as in **crew**. *The people who work on a ship are called its **crew**. **crew**.*

After your students have attempted the word **crew**, you show the ending **ew** written in green and then the beginning letters c-r written in black. They can see all four letters together that form the word **crew**.

● *The third word is **screw**. A screw has greater holding power than a nail. **screw**.*

This word contains a triple consonant blend. It also is liable to be missed by almost all your children. Don't worry about it. Before the year is out, all your children will automatically recognize the sound of **scr** and write **scr** when they hear it. Be

sure to point out the word **crew** is in **screw**.

*The fourth word for today is **brew**. We like to **brew** our own tea and coffee. **brew**.*

As you go through the procedure with **brew**, we recommend that you work through the word backwards! In other words, this time, ask what the last two letters are and then show -**ew**. On the dry erase board write **ew** in green (or whatever your favorite color is). Then ask what letter comes just before the sound of **ew**. Hopefully they will say "**r**" and you can write the **r** in black in front of the **ew**. Ask your children if they can hear the sound **rew** in the word **brew**. Ask for the first letter and then write the **b** in black in front of the **rew** to make **brew**.

*The fifth word for today is **drew**. Leonardo **drew** a picture of Mona. Or was it Lisa? **drew**.*

When they finish, ask for the last two letters and then write in green the letters **ew**. Ask for the letter that comes before the **ew**. Write the letter **r** in black to give **rew**. Ask your children if they can hear the sound **rew** in the word **drew**. Ask for the first letter and then write the **d** in black in front of the **rew** to make **drew**.

*The sixth word for today is **new**. Tell me something **new**. **new**.*

Your children should really get this word quickly, so you might just want to go to the next word quickly after writing **n** in black and **ew** in green to get **new**.

*The seventh word for today is **knew**. I just **knew** you would get the last word right. **knew**.*

If your children are puzzled as to the two "nooze" you can explain to them the problem of homophones. When you know that knowledge and knives and knights all start with a dumb k (dumb meaning silent and in slang also more than slightly stupid), you just laugh at our language but put in that silent k.

Continue giving the word, the sentence and the word again. After your children write the word, show the word correctly spelled with the ending family sound (the rime) in green and the initial consonants (onsets) in black. Let the children immediately correct any mistake before you go on to the next word.

8. **renew** Jason forgot to **renew** his library book. **renew**

9. **strew** You shouldn't **strew** your clohes all over the place. **strew**

10. **stew** There's nothing like a good Irish **stew** on a cold dreary day. **stew**

11. **dew*** I love to watch the sun sparkle off the morning **dew**. **dew**

12. **few** We will be finished with this lesson in just a **few** minutes. **few**

13. ***phew Phew**! Is it ever hot in here! **Phew** starts with a fancy PH! **phew**!

14. **nephew** Did you know Philip has a **nephew** older than he is? **nephew**

15. **spew** Wisecacks just **spew** out of David Letterman's mouth. **spew**

16. **aw Aw**, shucks. I'm sorry. **aw**

17. **law** How can it be against the **law** to tell the truth? **law**

18. **flaw** There has to be a **flaw** in your logic. **flaw**

19. **claw** She had to **claw** her way to the top. **claw**

20. **thaw** Grandma forgot to **thaw** out Grandpa's frozen dinner. **thaw**

21. **jaw** What kind of **jaw** bone did Samson use? **jaw**

22. **raw** You shouldn't eat **raw** meat. **raw**

23. **draw** You can **draw** your own conclusions. **draw**

24. **straw** Now, that's the last **straw**. **straw**

25. **paw** It's too bad that her little dog hurt its **paw**. **paw**

If you wish, you can tell your students that IF they have made all their corrections, they will receive an A on their papers. If one of them wrote *derw* for *drew* or for *drew* and failed to catch his mistake and correct it, you should NOT give him an A. Obviously, you don't want to give him an E, so don't give him anything except encouragement that tomorrow he will have a chance to do better and get an A. But make sure he corrects his misspelling. Don't just put a check mark. Have him erase *derw* or *brew* and have him correctly spell drew.

Second Day

Have your children take out their *AVKO Student Response Book for Sequential Spelling* and turn to page 5. Or, if you're using your own paper, have your children take out their spelling folders with the papers you had them carefully fold the day before. Have them go to the second sheet where you had them write Lesson 2. The purpose is to keep them from using the words that they had the day before as a mental crutch.

Obviously, if your children have *the AVKO Student Response Book for Sequential Spelling* this problem does not exist because the second day slot is on page 3, the third day is on page 5, the fourth day on page 7, the fifth day on page 9, etc. You can begin by telling your children, "Today, the first word is:

chews A cow **chews** its cud. **chews**

Notice it sounds the same as **choose**! Before you give the correct spelling, you might want to say something like: If I had said choose, Let's choose up sides, c-h-o-o-s-e would be the correct spelling. But I didn't say that. I said **chews** as in a cow **chews** its cud. **chews**. Do you know what the vowel sound is? It's ooooo as in a cow goes moo-o-o-o. What letters are we going to use for the "OO" sound? Write in green the **ew**. What's the last sound we hear? It's a z-z-z sound but we don't use the **z**. We use the letter **s** instead. Write the **s** in green. Then write the **ch** in black for the initial sound.-**chews**

2. ***crews** The foreman sent out three different work **crews** to get the job done. **crews**

Notice **crews** sounds the same as **cruise** Right from the beginning we will be showing the importance of the position of letters in words. Ask for the last letter first. If one of your children says "z" you know he has good hearing, but in our language we almost always use the letter s for the "z" sound when it makes a plural. We prefer that you don't bother with any formal grammatical explanation. Just have them write the s for the last letter. Then ask for the first letter. Most should be able to guess that the first letter is c as in cat. A "k" as in kitten is an intelligent error. Now ask what letter comes after the c and before the ooze sound that makes crews. Show the **r** in **cr** (both written in black) and then the **ews** written in green. If you wish you can also show them the other spelling of "krooz" which is **cruise**.

3. **screws**-You should have used brass **screws** instead of nails. **screws** Make sure you children see and hear the **crews** in **screws**.

4. **brews** I like the way my coffee maker **brews** my morning coffee. **brews (cf. bruise)**

5. **withdrew** The man **withdrew** $50.00 from his savings account. **withdrew**

6. **news**- Did you hear the latest news? **news**

7. **renews** Each year she **renews** her subscription to *The Reader's Digest*. **renews**

8. **strews** My sister **strews** peanut shells all over the floor. **strews**

9. **stews**-My neighbor sits and **stews** all day long over nothing. **stews**

10. **Jew** Did you know that Jesus Christ was a **Jew**? **Jew**

11. **fewer**-You are now making **fewer** mistakes in spelling.-**fewer**

12. ***phew Phew**! Is it ever hot in here. **phew**

Compare phew to few Although the first pronunciation given in the dictionary is the same as the word **few**, it is actually half word, half whistle in hwoooooohhh. We think all children should know both pronunciations. When phew is pronounced exactly the same as **few**, then it is easier, we think, to learn to spell **nephew. phew**

13. **nephews** I have seven **nephews** and seven nieces. **nephews**

14. **skews** Mr. Jones gives five times as many A's and B's as he does D's and E's and **skews** the normal curve. **skews**

15. **spews** Before a newly-drilled oil well is capped it **spews** oil all over the place. **spews**

16. ***awe** One should always be in **awe** of the power of God. Only God is truly awesome. **awe**

cf. aw-(cf. is the abbreviation for compare)

17. **laws** There are **laws** against just about everything **laws**

18. **flaws**-There are a number of **flaws** in your argument. **flaws**

19. ***claws** Jill doesn't have fingernails. They're more like **claws**. **claws**

cf. clause Claus

20. **thaws** If all this snow **thaws** quickly, we're liable to have a flood. **thaws**

21. **jaws** A German Shepherd has powerful **jaws**. **jaws**

22. **draws** Jack **draws** pictures as easily as other people doodle. **draws**

23. **straws** Jill likes to get extra **straws** when she drinks a soda. **straws**

24. ***paws** My cat's **paws** can really scratch. **paws**

cf. **pause**

25 **squaws**. Indian **squaws** performed many tasks essential to their tribe's survival. **squaws**

If you wish you can introduce (or re-introduce) your children to the concept of homophones. Many (if not most) elementary home school textbooks use the term homonyms which is technically incorrect. But who cares? Use whatever term you prefer.

Have each of your children correct his/her own paper. Make sure they erase any error and spell the word correctly. And please make sure that they try. Some children are so afraid of making a mistake that they will wait until you have written the correct spelling on the dry erase board before they write. Please, please, please don't let them do that. They will not learn if they simply copy correct spelling. They will learn only if they attempt to spell the word and then, and only then, correct any mistakes that they make.

The Third Day

We begin the third day by having the children take out their *AVKO Student Response Book for Sequential Spelling* or by having them take their spelling sheets from their special folder and going to the left hand column of the third sheet under the heading Lesson 3. We feel that it is easier to have your children open a response book to page 7 than it is to keep track of loose sheets of paper, but it can be done with the sheets successfully.

On this, the third day, you will begin the slow process of programming your children's God-given computer brains to form the ending -*ewed* correctly. There is no need at this time to encumber a child's mind with rules about doubling consonants whether the child is almost an adult or a second grader or somewhere in between. All we want to do is to have your children form the habit of spelling /ood/ -*ewed*. This way, when the rules for doubling letters are presented in their regular reading books, your children will find it easier to understand them. But, for now, please do not go into any lectures about short vowels and long vowels. It's not at all necessary. In fact, it generally tends to confuse children. However, if one of your precocious children asks about the rules, tell him that you will discuss the rules with him privately – and keep your word. You can start by saying:

1. **chewed** First he **chewed** up his food and then he swallowed it. **chewed**

2. ***knew** I just **knew** she would beat Jack up this hill. **knew**

3. **screwed** It took three teachers, but they **screwed** in the light bulb. **screwed**

4. ***brewed** The witches **brewed** up a magic potion. **brewed**

5. ***threw** The umpire **threw** Jill out of the game. **threw**

6. **newer** Our car may be old, but it's a lot **newer** than a Model T Ford. **newer**

7. **renewed** It seems like just yesterday that I got my license **renewed**. **renewed**

8. **strewed** The floor was **strewed** with popcorn and peanut shells. **strewed**

9. **stewed** She worried and **stewed** over how best to write the letter. **stewed**

10. **Jews** **Jews** have contributed greatly to western civilization. **Jews**

11. **fewest** I think Monaco has the **fewest** soldiers of any European country. **fewest**

12. ***few** Just a **few** people will spell **few** with a ph. **few**

13. **nephews** Both my **nephews** live in Philadelphia. **nephews**

14. **skewed** The normal curve was badly **skewed**. **skewed**

15. **spewed** The ruptured oil tanker **spewed** oil into the bay. **spewed**

16. **awful** It was just **awful**. **awful**

17. **lawful** Isn't it awful that adding an **l** makes **awful lawful**? **lawful**

18. **flawed** The material that was on sale was badly **flawed**. **flawed**

19. **thawed** We **thawed** the frozen meat first and then cooked it. **thawed**

20. **jawed** We **jawed** over the phone for about an hour or so. **jawed**

21. **drawn** We should have **drawn** a different picture. **drawn**

22. **drawer** We always keep a little extra cash hidden in a **drawer**. **drawer**

23. **pawed** The horse **pawed** the ground before he threw his rider. **pawed**

24. ***clawed** Have you ever been **clawed** by a cat? **clawed**

25. **drew** I **drew** an extra map for my nephew. **drew**

Homophones: knew / new / gnu I **knew** we were going to see the **new gnu** at the zoo. brewed / brood She **brewed** coffee for the entire **brood**. threw / through / THRU She **threw** the dart right **through** the **THRU** sign. clawed / Claude Our cat **clawed Claude.** Our cat named **Claude clawed** me.

The Fourth Day

The fourth day we begin by having the children take out their *AVKO Student Response Book for Sequential Spelling* and open it to page 9 or by having them take out their special spelling sheets and start on the fourth sheet, left hand column under Lesson Four.

1. **chewing** My dog really enjoys **chewing** on bones. **chewing**

2. **knew** I just **knew** you would spell one word starting with a **k. knew (cf. new & gnu)**

3. **screwing** Nailing boards together is okay but not as good as **screwing. screwing**

4. **brewing** Big black clouds are a sign that a storm is **brewing. brewing**

5. **blew** The wind was so strong it **blew** the roof off the barn. **blew (cf. blue)**

6. **newest** Of our three cars, our **newest** is a 1994 Chevrolet. **newest**

7. **renewing** It's a lot cheaper **renewing** books than paying library fines. **renewing**

8. **strewing** I got grounded once for **strewing** my clothes all over the floor. **strewing**

9. **stewing** When my aunt isn't fretting over something she's **stewing. stewing**

10. **Jewish** Nearly all of Jesus Christ's friends were **Jewish. Jewish**

11. **pew** Not everybody wants to sit in the front **pew. pew**

12. **few** Only my nephew will spell **few** with a ph. **few**

13. **nephew** Did you ever meet my **nephew** who is a minister? **nephew** before showing this, check your children's papers to see if they have learned to spell the word *nephew*. They probably spelled **nephew** correctly. Now, show them the misspellings you collected on the first day. Tell them you are proud of them. Tell them that they have learned a difficult word without ever having studied the

word. Tell them that just by paying attention in class and correcting their mistakes they are learning and learning a great deal.

14 **skewing** Statisticians know all about the **skewing** of averages. **skewing**

15. **spewing** I don't like to hear people **spewing** hateful ideas. **spewing**

16. **awfully** Sometimes it's **awfully** hard to figure these people out. **awfully**

17. **unlawful** In Michigan, it's **unlawful** to use foul language in public. **unlawful**

18. **flaws** When clothing manufacturers discover **flaws** in their goods, they very often sell them as seconds. **flaws**

19. **jawing** Bobby Joe is always **jawing** about something or other. **jawing**

20. **thawing** Grandma believes in **thawing** frozen meat in the refrigerator. **thawing**

21. **drawing** Have you ever noticed anyone **drawing** upside down? **drawing**

22. **drawers** My dad just built us a new chest of **drawers**. **drawers**

23. **pawing** The horse was so excited he kept **pawing** the ground. **pawing**

24. **clawing** Our cat is always **clawing** the furniture. **clawing**

25. **drew** We **drew** pictures of the pilgrims for Thanksgiving. **drew**

The Fifth Day

The fifth day we begin by having the children take out their *AVKO Student Response Book for Sequential Spelling* and open it to page 11 or by having them take out their special spelling sheets and starting on the fifth sheet, left hand column under Lesson 5.

1. **lawn** Who is supposed to mow the **lawn** today, Joe or Joanna? **lawn**

2. **pawn** In the game of chess, the **pawn** is expendable. **pawn**

3. **spawn** In the spring, the salmon swim upstream to **spawn**. **spawn**

4. **dawn** Both Don and Dawn do not like to get up at the crack of **dawn**. **dawn** (**Note**: In some dialects Don & Dawn are homophones, but not in Standard American English.)

5. **fawn** A baby deer is called a **fawn**. **fawn**

6. **yawn** Please don't **yawn**. It's contagious. **yawn**

7. **talk** The letters a-l in **talk** sound just like the letters a-w. **talk**

8. **stalk** Have you ever seen a celery **stalk**? **stalk**

9. **walk** Can you **walk** and chew bubble gum at the same time? **walk**

10. **sidewalk** You're supposed to walk on the **sidewalk**. **sidewalk**

11. **balk** Please don't **balk** at spelling **balk**. Pitchers sometimes **balk**. **balk**.

12. **chalk** I used to use **chalk** to write lessons on a blackboard. **chalk**

13. **calk** My great grandfather knew how to **calk** boats. **calk**

14. **caulk** Did you know that the most common spelling of **caulk** has a **u**? **caulk**

15. **milk** The **milk** we drink comes first from cows. **milk**

16. **silk** It's hard to make a **silk** purse out of a sow's ear. **silk**

17. **bilk** Sgt. Bilko used to try to **bilk** people out of their money. **bilk**

18. **hawk** Have you ever seen a **hawk** making lazy circles in the sky? **hawk**

19. **Mohawk** My great grandfather was a full blooded **Mohawk** Indian. **Mohawk**

20. *gawk* Why do motorists have to *gawk* at an accident? *gawk*

21. *awkward* Some beginning golfers take a very *awkward* swing. *awkward*

22. *sing* Can anyone *sing* a song of six pence? *sing*

23. **ring* A *ring* belongs on a finger. *ring*

24. **wring* My dad knows how to *wring* the water out of wet clothes. *wring*

25. *spring* My favorite time of the year is the *spring*. *spring*

The Sixth Day

We begin the sixth day by having the children take out their *AVKO Student Response Book for Sequential Spelling* and open it to page 13 or by having them take out their special spelling sheets and start on the back of the 1st sheet, left hand column under Lesson 6.

1. *lawns* My Uncle Tom makes a good living mowing *lawns*. *lawns*

2. *pawns* My Aunt Mary sacrificed two *pawns* for one bishop. *pawns*

3. *spawns* After the salmon *spawns*, they die. *spawns*

4. *dawns* I hope it finally *dawns* on him that there is hope after all. *dawns*

5. *fawns* I just love to take pictures of a doe and her *fawns*. *fawns*

6. *yawns* Every time someone *yawns*, I start to get sleepy myself. *yawns*

7. *talks* When everyone *talks* at once, nobody gets heard. *talks*

8. *stalks* I really love to eat *stalks* of celery with a cheese spread in them. *stalks*

9. *walks* My Uncle Larry *walks* to work every day. *walks*

10. *sidewalks* My Aunt Betsy shoveled the snow off *sidewalks* as a teenager. *sidewalks*

11. *balks* If a pitcher *balks*, the base runners can advance one base. *balks*

12. *chalks* When someone *chalks* up a loss to experience, he may be learning. *chalks*

13. *calks* When a carpenter repairs a broken window, he *calks* it. *calks*

Note: The preferred spelling of /kawk/ is "caulk."

14. *caulks* When Mr. Faulkner repairs a broken window, he *caulks* it. *caulks*

15. *milks* When a farmer *milks* a cow, he doesn't use the tail as a pump. *milks*

16. *silks* The finest of *silks* are made in China and Japan. *silks*

17. *bilks* When a salesman *bilks* a customer, he is cheating him. *bilks*

18. *hawks* Pray tell, are chicken *hawks* birds of prey? *hawks*

19. *Mohawks* Do you have any relatives who are *Mohawks*? I do. *Mohawks*

20. *gawks* When a motorist slows down and *gawks* at an accident, he might cause another accident. *gawks*

21. *awkwardly* Even the most graceful athletes sometimes do things *awkwardly*. *awkwardly*

22. *sings* If that thing *sings* another song, I will scream. *sings*

23. *rings* If the telephone *rings*, please answer it for me. *rings*

24. *wrings* When my father *wrings* out a wash cloth, it's almost dry. *wrings*

25. *springs* My folks bought a new set of box *springs* and a mattress. *springs*

The Seventh Day

The seventh day we begin by having the children take out their *AVKO Student Response Book for Sequential Spelling* and open it to page 15 or by having them take out their special spelling sheets and start on the back of the 2nd sheet, left hand column under Lesson 7.

1. *awning* My Uncle Richard put a new *awning* over the picture window. *awning*

2. *pawned* My Aunt May *pawned* her diamond bracelet for rent money. *pawned*

3. *spawned* The hurricane *spawned* a number of tornadoes. *spawned*

4. *dawned* It just *dawned* on him that he ought to pay attention. *dawned*

5. *fawned* It was disgusting the way the courtiers *fawned* over the king. *fawned*

6. *yawned* When you *yawned* it started everybody yawning. *yawned*

7. *talked* You should have *talked* to me first. *talked*

8. *stalked* The hunter *stalked* his prey for hours. *stalked*

9. *walked* We must have *walked* at least ten miles. *walked*

10. *walker* Is Mr. Walker a really fast *walker*? *walker*

11. *balked* Mr. Walker *balked* at giving us an extra day off for Easter. *balked*

12. *chalked* We *chalked* that up as being worth the try. *chalked*

13. **calked* Mr. Thomas *calked* his wooden row boat. *calked*

14. **caulked* Mr. Faulkner *caulked* his wooden row boat. *caulked*

15. *milked* The dairy farmer *milked* all his cows three times a day. *milked*

16. *silky* The dress was very *silky*. *silky*

17. *bilked* The crooked swindler *bilked* his own brother out of his money. *bilked*

18. *hawked* The salesman *hawked* his wares door to door. *hawked*

19. You say: "WUR GAW nuh WIN" Children spell: **We're going to win**

Your language books give explanations and rules about apostrophes. You don't need to interrupt the giving of the spelling words to give an explanation. All through this series and the following five series of AVKO Sequential Spelling Tests the -'s form is used with a word following it. The children's God-given computer brains will be properly programmed without rules being preached at them. However, if either you or your children want rules – give them the rules. That's all right, too.

20. *gawked* You really shouldn't have *gawked* at that poor man. *gawked*

21. Say: "YOR GONNA LOOZ" SPELL: **You're going to lose**.

22. *sang / sung* We *sang* the song that you should have *sung*. *sang / sung*

23. *rang / rung* We *rang* the bell after you had *rung* it twice. *rang / rung*

24. *wrung* He *wrung* all the water out of the wet rag. *wrung*

25. *sprang / sprung* He *sprang* to his feet when he should have *sprung*. *sprang / sprung*

After the Seventh Day

After the seventh day, I include a 25 word spelling test. Some days the tests are easier than others, but don't panic on days like the 126th day when the word *arrangements* is presented.

REMEMBER: My learning philosophy is *not* concerned about teaching the spelling of any one word *per se*. I am concerned with the teaching of basic sounds for both spelling and reading. In the case of words like *range, ranges, arrange, arranges, arrangement, arrangements*, I feel that teaching the *-ange* ending, the plural ending and the suffix *–ment,* as well as the initial consonant sounds and consonant blends, is important.

REMEMBER: Encourage your students to **speed** through these tests. Give the word. Put it in a sentence. Say the word. Spell the word. Have the students (if you can) trace the corrected spelling as they spell it aloud in group chorus. Go on to the next —but make sure your students make an attempt at the spelling *before* you give the correct spelling. **Copying** your spelling does **not** help them learn. **Correcting** their own misspelling **does**.

Immediate Feedback

The most common mistake made in administering the *AVKO Sequential Spelling Tests* is to give the entire test and then correct. This method just **won't** work.

● Give each word separately.

● Say the word. Give it in a sentence.

● Let the students attempt the spelling.

● Give the correct spelling. Let students correct their mistakes.

● Then give the next word. Repeat the process of immediate student self-correction.

Grading

If you desire to give grades for spelling, I would recommend that you give tests for grading purposes separately. You may then grade your students on their learning of the spelling of the sounds—not the words. Sequential Spelling gives permission for parents (and teachers) to duplicate (for their students only) the tests that come after the 40th, 80th, 120th, 160th and 180th days. Read the sentences to your students. All they have to do is fill in the blanks. Notice that you are not testing on the whole word. You are testing only on the spelling patterns taught. (That is why the initial consonants or blends are given to the student.) NOTE: You can use these as a pre-tests, as well as post-tests, to show progress. How you grade these tests is up to you. I recommend that 0-2 wrong = A, 3-4 = B, 5-6 = C, and 7-8 = D.

If your students get more than 8 wrong, I recommend going back over the process to help them learn what they are missing.

Questions most frequently asked concerning Sequential Spelling

1. What are those asterisks (*) and exclamation marks doing next to some words?

The asterisks merely serve as a reminder to the parent/teacher that the word so marked has a **homophone** (same pronunciation, different spelling), has a **heteronym** (same spelling, different word and different pronunciation), or does not follow the normal pattern. For

14

example, *gyp*** should logically be spelled "*jip.*"But instead of *j* we use the letter "*g.*" Instead of *i* the letter *y* is used. Likewise, the word *proper*** should logically be spelled "*propper*"just like *hopper*, and *copper*, and *stopper*, but it isn't.

2. Why don't the words used follow grade levels? For example, *nephew* is an *8th* grade word in many school's regular spelling texts.

Regular spelling texts, as a general rule, pick grade levels for words according to when the words first begin to occur in the curriculum. This would seem to make sense, but it does bring about some rather odd sequences. Since the word *ice* may not occur in the curriculum until the fourth grade (when it appears in the science class), its introduction is delayed until that time even though *nice* may occur in the first grade, *twice* in the second grade, *price* in the fifth, and *rice* in the sixth.

We believe in teaching the phonics necessary for decoding through the back door of spelling and without preaching rules that may or may not be useful. We teach the word *nephew* only after the *–ew* "*yoo*" sound has been taught in 12 different words. Notice that the word nephew is introduced directly after the homophones **few** and **phew**!

3. Why do you have so many words that are outside the vocabulary of normal adults, such as the word "mote"?

We don't believe it hurts anyone to learn a new word—but that is not why we use it. We use the word *mote* as an added practice in sounding out spellings of words having the initial /m/ sound and practice in spelling the ending *-ote*. It also gives the student a pleasant surprise and ego boost when he discovers he can spell a word that he believes he has never heard nor seen before—just because he knows how to spell the sounds.

4. Should I count off for sloppy handwriting?

Since the students get to correct their own spelling, they should be expected to write clearly and legibly. In fact, I recommend that these sequential spelling tests be used for handwriting practice because the patterns, being repetitive, can be a help in developing legible handwriting. I further recommend that if your students print, that they use D'Nealian® manuscript. If your students write, we strongly recommend D'Nealian® cursive. Another excellent system is the Italic by Getty-Dubay. But whatever system you use, we believe that **writing must be legible**. So, yes, by all means, take off for sloppy handwriting (provided the student has no physical disability and has sufficient small motor skills to write legibly).

5. Do I have to use all the words that are in the tests? Can I drop some? Can I change some?

No, you don't have to use them all. And yes, you can drop some. You know your children better than I do. Yes, you can substitute other words for the ones I have selected. *The Patterns of English Spelling* is your best reference to select from. If, for example, you would rather start with the -at, bat, rat, cat, sat family, be my guest. You can use your pencil to write in your choices. Every student is different. Don't be afraid to trust your own judgment.

6. Can I give the same test more than once during the day?

Yes. If your students can profit from that, fine. I recommend, however, that you allow a minimum of two hours to pass between re-tests. I also recommend four as the absolute maximum number of times that Sequential Spelling be given in one day, whether repeats or new lessons.

7. I have a child who is a 5th grader. May I use Sequential Spelling 1 to start one hour, Sequential Spelling 2 to start the 2nd hour, 3 for the third, etc.? I want my child to become as good a reader and speller as possible.

Why not? If it works, it works. If it doesn't, then try something else. You could try going through four days of Sequential Spelling I every day until it is finished and then move through four days of Sequential Spelling II every day, and continue on through four levels of Sequential Spelling in one year.

8. Why are some words in bold print?

The words in **bold print** are those that are the most commonly used words and the most important to learn. You will also notice that some words (like the word **doesn't**) that don't follow regular patterns are repeated many times throughout the series. If your students learn to spell any of the words that are not in bold face, that is a bonus. What I want the students to learn is to spell the most common words and to learn the most common patterns that occur in words. You will discover that most of these patterns consist of only two, three, or four letters. A big word like *misunderstandings* can be broken into the following patterns: *mis/un/der/st/and/ing/s*.

9. Do I have to teach all the homophones and homographs listed?

Absolutely not. I have listed them for your convenience. If you wish to teach them, fine. If you don't, fine. I only ask that when they come up that you definitely use the word in a sentence that helps the student pick the right word. For example: Don't just say **billed**. The students may think about the word **build**. Instead, say something like: "**billed**. *We were* **billed** *for extra carpeting.* **billed**.*"*

10. What does TPES stand for at the bottom of the pages?

TPES stands for *The Patterns of English Spelling*. This book contains all the words that share a common spelling pattern placed on the same page (or pages in the case of families like the -tion family). In our Sequential Spelling Series, I list most of the words in each family, but not all. If a parent/teacher wants to include more or wants to give special assignments to the gifted students, I have included the page references. This book may be purchased from the AVKO Educational Research Foundation, 3084 W. Willard Rd., Birch Run, MI 48415. For more information call toll free: 1-866-AVKO 612.

11. Can I use the words in Sequential Spelling for composition?

Yes, of course. Having your students create sentences out of the words is good exercise for their minds and will allow you to determine if they truly understand what the words really mean. You may also have them write the entire sentence that you dictate. That will help you help them handle the problems created by speech patterns, such as the "wanna" instead of "want to" and the "whacha gonna" for "what are you going to," etc. As the parent/teacher, you know your students and how many sentences they can handle as homework. You might even want to set time limits such as: Write as many sentences using today's spelling words as you can in 10 minutes.

12. Is there anything I can use to help my students' reading that will also reinforce the spelling?

AVKO's *New Word Families in Sentence Context* may be used in conjunction with Sequential Spelling. The page number given for *The Patterns of English Spelling* (TPES) also works for the *Word Families in Sentence Context*. This book may also be obtained from the AVKO Educational Research Foundation.

13. What if all my questions have not been answered here?

You can E-mail the author Don McCabe at info@avko.org or call 1-866-AVKO-612.

	1st day	2nd day	3rd day	4th day
1.	* **chew**	* **chews**	chewed	chewing
2.	crew	* **crews**	I **knew** it.	We knew it.
3.	screw	screws	screwed	screwing
4.	brew	* **brews**	* **brewed**	brewing
5.	**drew**	withdrew	I * **threw** it.	We * **blew** it.
6.	* **new**	news	newer	newest
7.	renew	renews	renewed	renewing
8.	strew	strews	strewed	strewing
9.	stew	stews	stewed	stewing
10.	dew	Jew	Jews	Jewish
11.	* **few**	fewer	fewest	pew
12.	* phew	! Phew	just a few	few
13.	**nephew**	nephews	nephews	nephew
14.	skew	skews	skewed	skewing
15.	spew	spews	spewed	spewing
16.	aw	awe	**awful**	**awfully**
17.	**law**	laws	lawful	unlawful
18.	flaw	flaws	flawed	flaws
19.	claw	* **claws**	* **clawed**	clawing
20.	thaw	thaws	thawed	thawing
21.	**jaw**	jaws	jawed	jawing
22.	**draw**	draws	drawn	drawing
23.	straw	straws	drawer	drawers
24.	paw	* **paws**	pawed	pawing
25.	squaw	squaws	drew	drew

* **Homophones:**

chew/choo	You can chew gum when you are on a "choo-choo" train.
chews/choose	He chews bubble gum instead of tobacco. Let's choose up sides.
crews/cruise	We have four different work crews. I love my cruise control when I drive.
brews/bruise	A brewer brews beer in a brewery. How did you get that bruise on your arm?
brewed/brood	The cook brewed some coffee. You don't have to sit and brood all day.
new/knew/gnu	What's new? I thought you knew we just got our first gnu at the zoo.
through/threw	We are almost through. Who threw the ball?
thru	Highway sign painters often use the word thru for through.
blew/blue	The wind blew. The sky is blue.
few/phew	Win a few. Lose a few. Phew! That was close!
paws/pause	A cat walks on four paws. What is the pause that refreshes?
claws/clause	We had our cat's claws removed. A clause is part of a sentence.
clawed/Claude	The cat clawed the curtains to shreds. Have you met my friend Claude?
to/too/two	It's too bad the two boys had to stay after school.

See the complete -ew family on p. 316 in *The Patterns of English Spelling* (TPES); the -aw, p. 319.

	5th day	6th day	7th day	8th day
1.	**lawn**	lawns	awning	awnings
2.	pawn	pawns	pawned	pawning
3.	spawn	spawns	spawned	spawning
4.	**dawn**	dawns	dawned	dawning
5.	fawn	fawns	fawned	fawning
6.	yawn	yawns	yawned	yawning
7.	**talk**	talks	**talked**	talking
8.	stalk	stalks	stalked	stalking
9.	**walk**	walks	walked	**walking**
10.	sidewalk	sidewalks	walker	walkers
11.	balk	balks	balked	balking
12.	chalk	chalks	chalked	chalking
13.	* **calk**	calks	calked	calked
14.	* **caulk**	caulks	caulked	caulked
15.	**milk**	milks	milked	milking
16.	**silk**	silks	silky	silkiest
17.	bilk	bilks	bilked	bilking
18.	hawk	hawks	hawked	hawking
19.	Mohawk	Mohawks	**We're** going to win.	**They're** coming.
20.	gawk	gawks	gawked	gawking
21.	awkward	awkwardly	You're going to lose.	**He's** going.
22.	**sing**	sings	sang/sung	singing
23.	* **ring**	rings	rang/rung	ringing
24.	* **wring**	wrings	*** wrang/wrung	wringing
25.	**spring**	springs	sprang/sprung	springing

* Homophones:

ring/wring   Put that ring on your finger or I'll wring your neck.
calk/caulk   You can calk around the windows or caulk around the windows. Your choice.

*** NOTE: The past tense of wring is wrung. However, since the past tense of ring is rang, and the past tense of spring is either spring or sprung, it's understandable that many children might use the non-standard wrang as the past tense of wrung.

See the complete -awn family on p. 423 in *The Patterns of English Spelling* (TPES);
        the -awk, p. 410; the -alk, p. 410; the -ilk, p. 245; -ing, p. 218.

Note: The preferred spelling of /kawk/ is caulk.

18

	9th day	10th day	11th day	12th day
1.	cling	clings	clung	clinging
2.	fling	flings	flung	flinging
3.	sling	slings	slung	slinging
4.	**string**	strings	strung	stringing
5.	**bring**	brings	brang/brought	bringing
6.	wing	**wings**	winged	winging
7.	swing	swings	swang/swung	**swinging**
8.	ping	pings	pinged	pinging
9.	ding	dings	dinged	dinging
10.	sting	stings	stung	stinging
11.	**thing**	things	stinger	stingers
12.	anything	everything	**nothing**	nothing
13.	king	kings	**again**	again
14.	lung	lungs	**against**	against
15.	dung	gung ho	**any**	anybody
16.	tone	tones	toned	toning
17.	**stone**	stones	stoned	stoning
18.	**bone**	bones	boned	boning
19.	cone	cones	boner	bony
20.	* **lone**	lonely	* **alone**	lonesome
21.	clone	clones	cloned	cloning
22.	cyclone	cyclones	zone	zones
23.	**tune**	tunes	tuned	tuning
24.	attune	attunes	attuned	attuning
25.	immune	immunity	immunize	immunization

* Homophones:

loan/lone   The Lone Ranger couldn't get a loan.
a loan/alone   He was all alone when he went for a loan.

See the complete -ing family on p. 218 in *The Patterns of English Spelling* (TPES);
the -ung, p. 219; the -one, p. 339; the -une, p. 340.

Note: Even though we conjugate the verb ring as ring, rang, rung, we should not conjugate bring as bring, brang, brung. It's bring, brought, brought. Likewise, with swing. It's not swing, swang, swung. It's properly swing, swung, swung.

	13th day	14th day	15th day	16th day
1.	prune	prunes	pruned	pruning
2.	dune	dunes	Neptune	Neptune's
3.	commune	comm**unity**	communities	communion
4.	opportune	**opportunity**	opportunities	opportunity
5.	* **Bob**	Bob's	Bobby	Bobby's
6.	* **bob**	bobs	bobbed	bobbing
7.	cob	cobs	gob	gobs
8.	lob	lobs	lobbed	lobbing
9.	blob	blobs	lobby	lobbies
10.	slob	slobs	knob	knobs
11.	mob	mobs	mobbed	mobbing
12.	**rob**	robs	**robbed**	robbing
13.	robber	robbers	robbery	robberies
14.	throb	throbs	throbbed	throbbing
15.	**hope**	hopes	hoped	**hoping**
16.	dope	dopes	doped	doping
17.	lope	lopes	loped	loping
18.	mope	mopes	moped	moping
19.	elope	elopes	eloped	eloping
20.	slope	slopes	sloped	sloping
21.	**rope**	ropes	roped	roping
22.	grope	gropes	groped	groping
23.	cope	copes	coped	coping
24.	**scope**	scopes	scoped	scoping
25.	telescope	telescopes	microscope	microscopes

* Homophones:

Bob/bob Bob used to love to bob for apples.

Note: *hoped* and *hoping* are often misspelled as *hopped* and *hopping* and vice versa.

See the complete -une family on p. 340 in *The Patterns of English Spelling* (TPES); the -ob, p. 104; the -ope, p. 342.

	17th day	18th day	19th day	20th day
1.	**back**	backs	backed	backing
2.	hack	hacks	hacked	hacking
3.	jack	jacks	jacked	jacking
4.	hijack	hijacks	hijacked	hijacking
5.	hacker	hackers	hijacker	hijackers
6.	lack	* **lacks**	lacked	**lacking**
7.	**black**	blacks	blacker	blackest
8.	slack	slacks	slacked	slacking
9.	clack	clacks	clacked	clacking
10.	snack	snacks	snacked	snacking
11.	**pack**	**packs**	* **packed**	**packing**
12.	unpack	unpacks	unpacked	unpacking
13.	repack	repacks	repacked	repacking
14.	tack	* **tacks**	* **tacked**	tacking
15.	stack	stacks	stacked	stacking
16.	rack	racks	racked	racking
17.	**track**	**tracks**	* **tracked**	tracking
18.	crack	cracks	**cracked**	cracking
19.	attack	attacks	**attacked**	attacking
20.	**stack**	stacks	stacked	stacking
21.	shack	shacks	**cracker**	**crackers**
22.	smack	smacks	smacked	smacking
23.	quack	quacks	quacked	quacking
24.	**sack**	* **sacks**	sacked	sacking
25.	whack	whacks	whacked	whacking

* Homophones:

lacks/lax	He lacks discipline. She is lax about enforcing rules.
tacks/tax	Is there a tax on thumb tacks?
packed/pact	They packed a whole lot of items in their pact for peace.
tacked/tact	He didn't show any tact when he tacked his poster over his opponent's.
tracked/tract	We tracked the animals on a lonely tract of land.
sacks/sax	We bought two sacks of groceries and a new sax.

See the complete -act family on p. 223 in *The Patterns of English Spelling* (TPES).

	21st day	22nd day	23rd day	24th day
1.	* **check**	checks	checked	**checking**
2.	deck	decks	decked	decking
3.	**neck**	necks	checker	**checkers**
4.	peck	pecks	pecked	pecking
5.	heck	reckless	recklessly	**wrecker**
6.	wreck	* **wrecks**	**wrecked**	wrecking
7.	fleck	flecks	flecked	flecking
8.	**sick**	sickly	sickest	sickness
9.	**lick**	licks	**licked**	licking
10.	slick	slicks	slicked	slicking
11.	flick	flicks	flicked	flicking
12.	flicker	flickers	flickered	flickering
13.	**click**	clicks	**clicked**	clicking
14.	**kick**	kicks	kicked	kicking
15.	nick	* **nicks**	nicked	nicking
16.	knickknack	knickers	kicker	kickers
17.	**pick**	* **picks**	picked	picking
18.	Rick	Rick's	clicker	clickers
19.	**trick**	**tricks**	tricked	tricking
20.	brick	bricks	bricked	bricking
21.	tick	ticks	ticked	ticking
22.	**stick**	sticks	stuck	sticking
23.	wick	wicks	chick	chicks
24.	**quick**	quicker	quickest	quickly
25.	Dick	* **Dick's**	**chicken**	chickens

* Homophones:

check/cheque	He wrote a check to pay for a Traveller's Cheque.
wrecks/Rex	Rex had two wrecks last month.
picks/pyx	A priest picks a pyx in which to place the consecrated host.
nicks/nix/Nick's	Nick's mother said nix to placing nicks in the police car's door.
Dick's/Dix	Dick's camp is Camp Dix.
Dick's son/Dixon	Dick's son married a Dixon girl.

See the complete -eck family on p. 215 in *The Patterns of English Spelling* (TPES); the -awk, p. 410.

	25th day	26th day	27th day	28th day
1.	* **ax**	axes	axed	axing
2.	**ask**	**asks**	**asked**	**asking**
3.	* **axe**	climax	flax	Max
4.	* **lax**	* **sax**	saxophone	saxophones
5.	**relax**	relaxes	relaxed	relaxing
6.	**wax**	waxes	**waxed**	waxing
7.	**six**	sixes	sixty	sixteen
8.	* **mix**	**mixes**	**mixed**	**mixing**
9.	**fix**	fixes	**fixed**	**fixing**
10.	prefix	prefixes	sixth	* **nix**
11.	suffix	suffixes	pixie	pixies
12.	mixer	mixers	mixture	mixtures
13.	* **Dix**	Dixie	fixture	fixtures
14.	* **coax**	coaxes	coaxed	coaxing
15.	hoax	hoaxes	hoaxed	hoaxing
16.	* **box**	boxes	**boxed**	**boxing**
17.	fox	foxes	foxed	foxing
18.	outfox	outfoxes	outfoxed	outfoxing
19.	* **sox**	* **lox**	Mr. Cox	pox
20.	ox	oxen	* **phlox**	smallpox
21.	**fast**	fasts	fasted	fasting
22.	breakfast	* **mast**	masts	in the * **past**
23.	cast	casts	casters	casting
24.	broadcast	broadcasts	broadcasted	broadcasting
25.	**last**	lasts	lasted	lasting

* Homophones:

ax/axe	Lizzie Borden took an ax (axe) and gave her mother forty whacks.
sax/sacks	Tom plays the sax. His brother plays with sacks and boxes.
lax/lacks	Lax law enforcement lacks the ability to control.
mix/Mick's	Mick's mother used to mix us up.
nix/Nick's/nicks	Nick's dad said nix to putting nicks in anything.
coax/cokes	We used to coax our folks for extra cokes.
box/Bach's	We have some of Bach's music in a box in the attic.
sox/socks	He bought a pair of sox. She bought a pair of socks.
past/passed	In the past, students were passed despite their failing grades.
mast/massed	The sailors massed around the mast.
Dix/Dick's	Dick's wife is Marilyn Dix.
lox/locks/loughs	You can eat lox, use locks, and swim in Irish loughs.
phlox/flocks	Shepherds herd flocks of sheep. Phlox are flowers.

See the complete -ax family on p. 265 in *The Patterns of English Spelling* (TPES);
the -ix, p. 267; the -ox, p. 268; the -oax, p. 268; -ast, p. 233.

29th day	30th day	31st day	32nd day
1. blast	blasts	blasted	blasting
2. vast	vastly	yeast	anymore
3. **east**	eastern	northeast wind	easterly
4. Easter	Easterner	the Northeast	the Southeast
5. feast	feasts	feasted	feasting
6. **beast**	beasts	**at least**	southeast wind
7. **Christ**	Christ's	**Christmas**	Xmas
8. **Christian**	Christians	persistent	existence
9. **Christianity**	consistent	consistently	persistently
10. **list**	lists	listed	listing
11. enlist	enlists	enlisted	enlisting
12. **assist**	assists	assisted	assisting
13. insist	insists	**insisted**	insisting
14. consist	consists	consisted	consisting
15. persist	persists	persisted	persisting
16. resist	resists	resisted	resisting
17. *** mist**	mists	misted	misting
18. **twist**	twists	twisted	twisting
19. whist	assistant	*** assistants**	*** assistance**
20. grist	insistent	persistent	resistance
21. **exist**	exists	existed	existing
22. **boast**	boasts	boasted	boasting
23. **coast**	coasts	coasted	coaster
24. **roast**	roasts	roaster	roasting
25. **toast**	toasted	toasting	toaster

* Homophones:

assistants/assistance   The two assistants gave the doctor assistance.
mist/missed   We missed the heavy mist of London.

Note: The X in Christmas comes from the
Greek letter X that the word Christ in Greek begins with.

See the complete -ast family on p. 233 in *The Patterns of English Spelling* (TPES);
the -east, p. 237; the -ist, p. 235; the -oast, p. 235.

	33rd day	34th day	35th day	36th day
1.	**lost**	lost	lost	lost
2.	**cost**	costs	costly	frosty
3.	accost	accosts	accosted	accosting
4.	**frost**	frosts	frosted	frosting
5.	defrost	defrosts	defrosted	defrosting
6.	* **must**	musty	* **mustard**	custard
7.	**dust**	dusts	dusted	dusting
8.	**just**	justly	dusty	duster
9.	adjust	adjusts	adjusted	adjusting
10.	readjust	readjusts	readjusted	readjusting
11.	gust	gusts	gusted	gusting
12.	disgust	disgusts	**disgusted**	disgusting
13.	rust	rusts	rusted	rusting
14.	crust	crusts	crusty	trusty
15.	* **trust**	trusts	trusted	trusting
16.	thrust	thrusts	thrust	thrusting
17.	* **bust**	busts	busted	busting
18.	robust	burst	bursts	bursting
19.	beam	beams	beamed	beaming
20.	ream	reams	reamed	reaming
21.	**cream**	creams	creamed	creaming
22.	**scream**	screams	screamed	screaming
23.	**dream**	dreams	dreamed	dreaming
24.	**stream**	streams	streamed	streaming
25.	**steam**	steams	steamed	steaming

* Homophones:

must/mussed	He must go. He mussed up his hair.
trust/trussed	We trust you. Make sure he is trussed up tightly.
bust/bussed	The police made a bust. The children were bussed to school.
mustard/mustered	I like catsup and mustard. He was mustered out of the army.

See the complete -ost family on p. 235 in *The Patterns of English Spelling* (TPES);
the -ust, p. 236; the -eam, p. 418.

	37th day	38th day	39th day	40th day
1.	**team**	teams	teamed	* **teaming**
2.	steam	steams	steamed	steaming
3.	* **seam**	seams	seamstress	seamstresses
4.	gleam	gleams	gleamed	gleaming
5.	squeamish	creamer	creamery	dreamers
6.	streamer	streamers	steamer	screamer
7.	lame	**came**	became	overcame
8.	**blame**	blames	blamed	blaming
9.	flame	**flames**	flamed	flaming
10.	fame	fame	famous	famously
11.	**game**	games	James	**ashamed of**
12.	**name**	names	named	naming
13.	nickname	nicknames	nicknamed	nicknaming
14.	surname	surnames	tame	tamely
15.	**shame**	shames	shamed	shaming
16.	dame	dames	**ashamed**	ashamed
17.	frame	frames	framed	framing
18.	hem	hems	hemmed	hemming
19.	Aunt Em	Auntie Em	Clem	Clem's aunt
20.	**them**	gem	themselves	them
21.	stem	stems	stemmed	stemming
22.	gem	gems	long-stemmed	condem**n**ation
23.	*** condem**n**	condem**n**s	condemned	condemning
24.	**from**	from	from	from
25.	Tom	mom	*** **bomb**	bom**b**s

* Homophones:

seam/seem	He ripped out the seam in his shirt. It would seem that it wasn't good enough for him.
teaming/teeming	They were teaming up against us. The pond was teeming with fish.
bomb/balm	Applying balm to itchy or chapped skin is soothing. A bomb isn't.

*** NOTE: There is a silent n at the end of condemn and a silent b at the end of bomb. See section on silent letters in *The Patterns of English Spelling*, pp. 958-961.

See the complete -eam family on p. 418 in *The Patterns of English Spelling* (TPES);
the -ame, p. 332; the -em, p. 117; the -om, p. 119.

Evaluation Test #1 (After 40 Days)

		Pattern being tested	Lesson word is in
1.	Not all Irishmen love an Irish st**ew**.	ew	1
2.	I have all kinds of nieces and neph**ews**.	ews	2
3.	I wouldn't want to live in a house made of str**aw**.	aw	1
4.	It's awfully sloppy when it's th**awing** outside.	awing	4
5.	It d**awned** on me that today's the day for a test.	awned	7
6.	The Moh**awks** are a proud tribe of American Indians.	awks	6
7.	They're always s**inging** songs.	inging	8
8.	Rolling st**ones** gather no moss.	ones	10
9.	Musicians are good at t**uning** their instruments.	uning	12
10.	They keep complaining that they were r**obbed**.	obbed	15
11.	We were h**oping** that they would grow up.	oping	16
12.	The auditorium was just jam-p**acked** with people.	acked	19
13.	I enjoy a good game of ch**eckers** once in a while.	eckers	24
14.	You shouldn't have k**icked** him in the shins.	icked	23
15.	I **asked** him to please behave.	asked	27
16.	Perry Como is always very rel**axed**.	axed	27
17.	The program l**asted** for only twenty minutes.	asted	27
18.	I thought it would last for at l**east** thirty.	east	31
19.	We bought them a t**oaster** for their wedding present.	oaster	32
20.	We were disg**usted** with their selfish behavior.	usted	35

Name_____ Date_____

Evaluation Test #1

Please, please, please do NOT start until the directions are given.

Wait until the sentences are read before you begin filling in the blanks with the missing letters.

1. Not all Irishmen love an Irish st_____.

2. I have all kinds of nieces and neph_____.

3. I wouldn't want to live in a house made of str_____.

4. It's awfully sloppy when it's th_____ outside.

5. It d_____ on me that today's the day for a test.

6. The Moh_____ are a proud tribe of American Indians.

7. They're always s_____ songs.

8. Rolling st_____ gather no moss.

9. Musicians are good at t_____ their instruments.

10. They keep complaining that they were r_____.

11. We were h_____ that they would grow up.

12. The auditorium was just jam p_____ with people.

13. I enjoy a good game of ch_____ once in a while.

14. You shouldn't have k_____ him in the shins.

15. I _____ him to please behave.

16. Perry Como is always very rel_____.

17. The program l_____ for only twenty minutes.

18. I thought it would last for at l_____ thirty.

19. We bought them a t_____ for their wedding present.

20. We were disg_____ with their selfish behavior.

	41st day	42nd day	43rd day	44th day
1.	**faith**	faithful	faithfully	faithfulness
2.	**math**	unfaithful	unfaithfully	unfaithfulness
3.	**bath**	baths	path	paths
4.	bathe	bathes	bathed	bathing
5.	**path**	paths	warpath	warpaths
6.	aftermath	lath	wrath	Miss Rath
7.	**father**	fathers	fathered	fathering
8.	**mother**	mothers	mothered	mothering
9.	smother	smothers	smothered	smothering
10.	**brother**	brothers	stepbrother	stepfather
11.	bother	bothers	bothered	bothering
12.	**south**	in the South	**with**	**without**
13.	mouth	mouths	**anyplace**	**anything**
14.	Beth	Beth's breath	**aren't**	**hadn't**
15.	**death**	deaths	**my * aunt**	*** aunts**
16.	**breath**	breaths	*** Aunt** Mary	my * **aunt's** hat
17.	breathe	breathes	breathed	breathing
18.	**cloth**	cloths	because	because
19.	clothe	*** clothes**	clothed	clothing
20.	**health**	healthy	healthier	healthiest
21.	**wealth**	wealthy	wealthier	wealthiest
22.	bum	bums	bummed	bumming
23.	*** sum**	sums	summed	summing
24.	**gum**	gums	summary	summaries
25.	hum	hums	hummed	humming

* Homophones:

clothes/close	I love to buy new clothes. Will you close the door, please.
sum/some	He won a vast sum of money. I would like some of his luck.
ant/aunt/Aunt Mary	My Aunt Mary was bitten by a fire ant. Is your aunt coming to the party?
ants/aunts/aunt's	She used her aunt's collection of ants as a science project.
aftermath/after math	The aftermath of the argument after math class is still undetermined.

See the complete -aith family on p. 278 in *The Patterns of English Spelling* (TPES);
the -ath, p. 275; the -eath, p. 275; the -eathe, p. 279; -oth, p. 218; -othe, 279;
-athe, p. 279; -ealth, p. 280; -um, p. 120.

	45th day	46th day	47th day	48th day
1.	**drum**	drums	drummed	drumming
2.	chum	chums	chummed	chumming
3.	* **plum**	plums	drummer	drummers
4.	* **plumb**	plumbs	plumbed	plumbing
5.	**crumb**	**crumbs**	plumber	plumbers
6.	**thumb**	**thumbs**	thumbed	thumbing
7.	**dumb**	dumber	dumbest	dumb
8.	slum	slums	slummed	slumming
9.	glum	mum	mums	**I'd**
10.	scum	yum	* **clothes**	* **clothes**
11.	autumn	autumns	**aren't**	aren't
12.	column	columns	**hadn't**	**doesn't**
13.	* **son**	sons	bacon	dragon
14.	ton	tons	* **won**	wagon
15.	**common**	commonly	uncommon	uncommonly
16.	**gallon**	gallons	sermon	sermons
17.	bun	buns	bunny	bunnies
18.	gun	guns	gunned	gunning
19.	**fun**	**funny**	funnier	funniest
20.	stun	stuns	stunned	**stunning**
21.	**shun**	**shuns**	**shunned**	**shunning**
22.	* **sun**	suns	sunned	sunning
23.	**run**	runs	**ran**	**running**
24.	* **nun**	nuns	runner	**runners**
25.	* **none**	**no one**	**none**	**none**

*Homophones:

plum/plumb	He ate an apple, a pear, and a plum. She knows how to use a plumb bob.
close/clothes	Please close the clothes closet door.
sun/son	The sun is up. Their son is still in bed.
nun/none	The nun won none of the money.
one/won	Who was the one who won the money?

> **Note**: These are the only words in which the sound /shun/ is spelled shun. All other times the sound /shun/ is spelled one of three ways: tion as in nation; ssion as in mission; cion as in suspicion.

See the complete -um family on p. 120 in *The Patterns of English Spelling* (TPES); the -umb, p. 120; the -on, pp. 124, 835-851; the -un, p. 125.

49th day	50th day	51st day	52nd day
1. pardon	pardons	pardoned	pardoning
2. London	lesson	lessons	**aren't**
3. poison	poisons	poisoned	poisoning
4. weapon	weapons	*** clothes**	*** clothes**
5. **iron**	irons	ironed	ironing
6. **reason**	reasons	reasoned	reasoning
7. treason	because	**I'd**	**because**
8. **season**	seasons	seasoned	seasoning
9. arson	many	**many**	**many**
10. parson	parsons	**says**	**says**
11. **prison**	prisons	prisoner	prisoners
12. **ton**	tons	*** I'll**	*** I'll**
13. carton	cartons	island	*** isle**
14. melon	melons	felon	felons
15. pun	puns	punned	punning
16. spun	Hun	Huns	**island**
17. * dun	duns	dunned	dunning
18. * **done**	all done	well done	poorly **done**
19. **sir**	sirs	*** fir**	**firs**
20. **stir**	stirs	**stirred**	**stirring**
21. whir	whirs	whirred	whirring
22. **her**	hers	**herself**	*** were**
23. refer	refers	**referred**	**referring**
24. **prefer**	prefers	**preferred**	preferring
25. **offer**	offers	offered	**offering**

* Homophones:

clothes/close	We need some new clothes. What time does the store close?
I'll/isle/aisle	I'll need a boat to go to that isle. Have you been down the aisle?
fir/fur	You don't get fur from a fir tree.
done/dun/Dunn/Donne	When you're done collecting, please don't dun Irene Dunne or John Donne.
were/we're	Where were you? We're going to win.

See the complete -on family on pp. 835-851 in *The Patterns of English Spelling* (TPES); the -un, p. 125; the -ir, p. 514; the -er, p. 511.

	53rd day	54th day	55th day	56th day
1.	differ	differs	differed	differing
2.	**different**	differently	difference	differences
3.	suffer	suffers	suffered	**suffering**
4.	confer	confers	conferred	conferring
5.	* **infer**	infers	inferred	inferring
6.	transfer	transfers	transferred	transferring
7.	**cool**	cools	cooled	cooling
8.	fool	fools	fooled	**fooling**
9.	pool	pools	pooled	pooling
10.	spool	spools	spooled	spooling
11.	tool	**tools**	tooled	tooling
12.	drool	drools	drooled	drooling
13.	**school**	schools	schooled	schooling
14.	high school	grade school	unschooled	school age
15.	cab	cabs	lab	labs
16.	scab	scabs	slab	slabs
17.	blab	blabs	blabbed	blabbing
18.	flab	flabby	flabbier	flabbiest
19.	tab	tabs	tabbed	tabbing
20.	stab	stabs	stabbed	stabbing
21.	gab	gabs	gabbed	gabbing
22.	**grab**	grabs	grabbed	grabbing
23.	crab	crabs	grabby	grabbiest
24.	drab	drabs	**crabby**	crabbiest
25.	dab	dabs	dabbed	dabbing

* Homophones:

infer/in fur   I could infer that Eskimos are dressed in fur.

See the complete -er family on p. 511 in *The Patterns of English Spelling* (TPES);
the -ool, p. 414; the -ab, p. 101.

	57th day	58th day	59th day	60th day
1.	**food**	foods	* I'll	* were
2.	* **mood**	moods	moody	moodiest
3.	brood	broods	brooded	brooding
4.	fib	fibs	fibbed	fibbing
5.	bib	bibs	island	what
6.	rib	ribs	ribbed	ribbing
7.	crib	cribs	cribbed	cribbing
8.	lib	glib	squib	cribbage
9.	tub	tubs	rubber	rubbery
10.	stub	stubs	stubbed	stubbing
11.	dub	dubs	dubbed	dubbing
12.	cub	cubs	bub	chub
13.	nub	nubs	hubbub	chubby
14.	snub	snubs	snubbed	snubbing
15.	club	clubs	clubbed	clubbing
16.	flub	flubs	flubbed	flubbing
17.	**rub**	rubs	rubbed	rubbing
18.	scrub	scrubs	scrubbed	scrubbing
19.	drub	drubs	drubbed	drubbing
20.	grub	grubs	grubbed	grubbing
21.	shrub	shrubs	shrubbery	blubber
22.	sub	subs	subbed	subbing
23.	* **tea**	* **teas**	* **isle**	* **we're**
24.	* **pea**	* peas	* **sea**	* **seas**
25.	* **flea**	* **fleas**	plea	* **pleas**

* Homophones:

I'll/aisle/isle	I'll not go down any aisle on that isle.
we're/were	We're not interested in knowing where you were.
mood/mooed	I'm not in the mood to hear how the cow mooed.
tea/tee/ti/T	Drink your tea. In golf, you use a tee. Do, re, mi, fa, sol, la, ti, do. Q, R, S, T.
pleas/please	When she entered her client's pleas of not guilty, she said please.
sea/see/si	If you can see the sea, say, "Si!"
seas/sees/seize/C's	Oceans are bigger than seas. If he sees you, seize the moment.
tease/tees/teas	Don't tease me because I break so many golf tees or drink different teas.
were/we're	If you were paying attention, you'd know where we're going.
flea/flee	The bug spray made the flea flee.
pea/pee peas/pees	A pea is a vegetable. "Pee" is a "taboo" word for urine or urinate.

See the complete -ood family on p. 404 in *The Patterns of English Spelling* (TPES); the -ib, p. 103; the -ub, p. 105; the -ea, p. 305.

	61st day	62nd day	63rd day	64th day
1.	* **peace**	peaceful	peacefully	peaceful
2.	* **piece**	pieces	pieced	piecing
3.	niece	nieces	piecework	piecemeal
4.	**head**	heads	headed	heading
5.	forehead	foreheads	deadhead	deadheads
6.	* (**) **read**	redhead	blackhead	blackheads
7.	tread	treads	trod	treading
8.	treadle	treadles	downtrodden	**aren't**
9.	spread	spreads	spread	spreading
10.	* **bread**	breads	breaded	breading
11.	dread	dreads	dreaded	dreading
12.	stead	bedstead	dreadful	dreadfully
13.	steady	steadier	steadiest	steadily
14.	* (**) **lead**	pencil leads	**instead**	**doesn't**
15.	thread	threads	threaded	threading
16.	**voice**	voices	voiced	voicing
17.	invoice	invoices	invoiced	invoicing
18.	Joyce	Joyce's voice	choice	choices
19.	rejoice	rejoices	rejoiced	rejoicing
20.	void	voids	voided	voiding
21.	* **avoid**	avoids	avoided	avoiding
22.	asteroid	asteroids	devoid	Negroid
23.	**oil**	oils	oiled	oiling
24.	boil	boils	**boiled**	boiling
25.	broil	broils	broiled	broiling

* Homophones:

peace/piece	I can't rest in peace until I give them a piece of my mind.
read/red	Have you read *The Red Badge of Courage*?
lead/led	The trail of the lead pencil led to his arrest.
bread/bred	The love of baking bread is bred into bakers.
avoid/a void	What means to stay away from nothing? Avoid a void!

** Heteronyms:

read/read	Read me a book that you haven't already read to me.
lead/lead	Lead me on, MacDuff. Show me how to make gold from lead.

See the complete -iece family on p. 432 in *The Patterns of English Spelling* (TPES);
the -eace, p. 432; the -ead, p. 402; the -oice, p. 433; -oid, p. 403; -oil, 415.

	65th day	66th day	67th day	68th day
1.	foil	foils	foiled	foiling
2.	spoil	spoils	spoiled	spoiling
3.	toil	toils	toiled	toiling
4.	coil	coils	coiled	coiling
5.	recoil	recoils	recoiled	recoiling
6.	soil	soils	soiled	soiling
7.	turmoil	toilet	toilets	toiletry
8.	**join**	joins	joined	joining
9.	joint	joints	* **clothes**	**aren't**
10.	rejoin	rejoins	rejoined	rejoining
11.	coin	coins	coined	coining
12.	loin	loins	sirloin	sirloins
13.	tenderloin	tenderloins	groin	joiner
14.	**point**	points	pointed	pointing
15.	* **appoint**	appoints	appointed	appointing
16.	disappoint	disappoints	**disappointed**	disappointing
17.	anoint	anoint	anointed	anointing
18.	ointment	appointment	disappointment	* **I'll**
19.	**loud**	loudly	louder	loudest
20.	* **aloud**	proud	proudly	proudest
21.	**cloud**	clouds	clouded	clouding
22.	cloudy	cloudier	cloudiest	outloud
23.	shroud	shrouds	shrouded	shrouding
24.	crowd	crowds	crowded	crowding
25.	* **you**	* **you're** it	* **your** house	**says**

* Homophones:

a loud/aloud/allowed — Anyone with a loud voice should be allowed to read aloud.
appoint/a point — He made a point to appoint a woman as chairman of the board.
clothes/close — Please close the clothes closet door.
I'll/isle/aisle — I'll go down an aisle (in a store) on a misty isle (island).
you/ewe/U/yew — You should see a ewe make a U-turn around a yew.
your/you're — You're wanted at home. Your mother's calling.

See the complete -oil family on p. 415 in *The Patterns of English Spelling* (TPES); the -oin, p. 423; the -oint, p. 253; the -oud, p. 403; -owd, p. 403.

	69th day	70th day	71st day	72nd day
1.	**mouse**	**mice**	**I'd**	**because**
2.	louse	lice	**many**	**many**
3.	blouse	blouses	bloused	blousing
4.	douse	douses	doused	dousing
5.	** **house**	(n.) * **houses**	**because**	* **isle**
6.	to ** **house**	(v.) * **houses**	housed	**housing**
7.	louse up	louses up	loused up	lousing up
8.	youth	youthful	youthfulness	youths
9.	**save**	saves	saved	**saving**
10.	pave	paves	paved	paving
11.	**shave**	shaves	shaved	**shaving**
12.	rave	raves	raved	raving
13.	grave	graves	lifesaver	shaver
14.	engrave	engraves	engraved	engraving
15.	**brave**	braves	braved	braving
16.	braver	bravery	bravest	**bravely**
17.	**cave**	caves	caved	caving
18.	crave	craves	craved	craving
19.	**slave**	slaves	slaved	slaving
20.	slaver	slavery	**gave**	**forgave**
21.	* **wave**	waves	waved	waving
22.	* **waive**	waives	waived	waiving
23.	behave	behaves	behaved	behaving
24.	misbehave	misbehaves	misbehaved	misbehaving
25.	**have**	**haven't**	**having**	**haven't**

* Homophones:

wave/waive	Be careful or you'll waive your right to wave good-bye.
I'll/isle/aisle	I'll visit an isle, but I won't walk down the aisle.
houses/houses	A prison houses criminals in cells not houses.

** Heteronyms:

house ("HOW-zz")/house ("HOW-ss")You don't have to house a criminal in his own house.

See the complete -ouse family on p. 433 in *The Patterns of English Spelling* (TPES);
the -ave, p. 324.

36

	73rd day	74th day	75th day	76th day
1.	**safe**	safes	safety	safeties
2.	chafe	chafes	chafed	chafing
3.	strafe	strafes	strafed	strafing
4.	ravel	ravels	ravelled	ravelling
5.	unravel	unravels	raveled	raveling
6.	**travel**	**travels**	**traveled**	**traveling**
7.	**(Am.) traveler**	**travelers**	**travelled**	**travelling**
8.	**(Br.) traveller**	**travellers**	gavelled	gavelling
9.	gavel	gavels	gaveled	gaveling
10.	**life**	nine lives	lifelike	my life's work
11.	**wife**	wives	fife	fifes
12.	rife	I have	I've	I've
13.	strife	**two knives**	you've	*** we've**
14.	**knife**	**knifes**	knifed	knifing
15.	**** live**	**** lives**	lived	**living**
16.	relive	relives	relived	reliving
17.	olive	olives	liver	livers
18.	**give**	gives	gave	**giving**
19.	**** live** music	lively	alive	lively
20.	dive	dives	dived	diving
21.	drive	drives	drove	**driving**
22.	**five**	fives	diver	driver
23.	arrive	arrives	arrived	**arriving**
24.	revive	revives	revived	reviving
25.	survive	survives	survived	surviving

* Homophones:

we've/weave   We've learned how to weave.

** Heteronyms:

live ("liv")/live ("LYH'v")   I live to listen to live music.
lives("livz")/lives("LYH'vz") He lives alone and watches the TV show "Days of Our Lives."

> **NOTE:** The preferred American spelling has the single *l* in words such as *traveled*. British spelling always uses the double *l* as in *travelled*. Americans are tending to adopt this particular British habit.

See the complete -afe family on p. 324 in *The Patterns of English Spelling* (TPES);
the -ive, p. 325; the -ife, p. 325; the -ave, p. 324.

	77th day	78th day	79th day	80th day
1.	thrive	thrives	thrived	thriving
2.	deprive	deprives	deprived	depriving
3.	strive	strives	strived	striving
4.	**move**	moves	moved	**moving**
5.	remove	removes	removed	removing
6.	**prove**	proves	proved	**proving**
7.	approve	approves	**approved**	approving
8.	disapprove	disapproves	disapproved	disapproving
9.	**improve**	improves	improved	**improving**
10.	**movie**	movies	approval	improvement
11.	**am**	**I'm** going to go.	* **You're** going to go.	* **We're** going to go.
12.	ram	rams	rammed	ramming
13.	cram	crams	crammed	cramming
14.	scram	scrams	scrammed	scramming
15.	dram	drams	gram	grams
16.	pram	prams	tram	trams
17.	jam	jams	jammed	jamming
18.	bam	Sam-I-Am	cam	cams
19.	* **dam**	dams	dammed	damming
20.	* **damn**	damns	damned	damning
21.	ham	hams	hammed	hamming
22.	* **lam**	tam	sham	shams
23.	* **lamb**	lambs	wham	swam
24.	slam	slams	slammed	slamming
25.	clam	clams	clammed	clamming

*** Homophones:**

dam/damn	Never damn a dam. Dam a river instead.
lam/lamb	A man on the lam hasn't time to cook and eat lamb chops.
you're/your	You're going to get your answer soon enough.
We're/were	We're going to find out where you were.

NOTE: To *damn* is really short for *to condemn*. The **n** is silent in the short form but you hear it in the longer forms, dam**n**ation and condem**n**ation. Also: Please read the words *going to* as "gonna"! This "Scrunching up" in speech, common to all dialects, is a phenomenon known to linguists as synaloepha or sandhi.

See the complete -awn family on p. 423 in (TPES); the -awk, p. 410; -alk, p. 410; -ilk, p. 245; -ing, p. 218.

Evaluation Test #2
(After 80 Days)

		Pattern being tested	Lesson word is in
1.	The injured man scr**eamed** for help.	eamed	35
2.	You should be ash**amed** of yourself.	amed	39
3.	His f**ather** was a farmer.	ather	41
4.	Do you like liver sm**othered** in onions?	othered	43
5.	I would rather be h**ealthy** than to be sick.	ealthy	42
6.	I would rather hear him h**umming** than singing.	umming	44
7.	The whole team gave the th**umbs** up sign.	umbs	46
8.	The dress she wore to the awards show was st**unning**.	unning	48
9.	We donate our old cl**othes** to Good Will.	othes	52
10.	Do you know who st**irred** up all that trouble?	irred	51
11.	I don't pay any attention to cr**abby** people.	abby	55
12.	The doctor scr**ubbed** her hands before operating.	ubbed	59
13.	The sleeping child looked very p**eace**ful.	eace	62
14.	Why don't we just watch TV inst**ead**?	ead	63
15.	The cook specialized in b**oiling** water.	oiling	64
16.	I hope you're not disapp**ointed** in me.	ointed	67
17.	I hate people who are always cr**owding** me.	owding	68
18.	She bought two new bl**ouses** at Macy's.	ouses	70
19.	That kid is always misbeh**aving**.	aving	72
20.	Did you see anything new on your tr**avels**?	avels	74

Name_____ Date_____

Evaluation Test #2

1. The injured man scr_____ for help.

2. You should be ash_____ of yourself.

3. His f_____ was a farmer.

4. Do you like liver sm_____ in onions?

5. I would rather be h_____ than to be sick.

6. I would rather hear him h_____ than singing.

7. The whole team gave the th_____ up sign.

8. The dress she wore to the awards show was st_____.

9. We donate our old cl_____ to Good Will.

10. Do you know who st_____ up all that trouble?

11. I don't pay any attention to cr_____ people.

12. The doctor scr_____ her hands before operating.

13. The sleeping child looked very p_____ful.

14. Why don't we just watch TV inst_____?

15. The cook specialized in b_____ water.

16. I hope you're not disapp_____ in me.

17. I hate people who are always cr_____ me.

18. She bought two new bl_____ at Macy's.

19. That kid is always misbeh_____.

20. Did you see anything new on your tr_____?

	81st day	82nd day	83rd day	84th day
1.	* **him**	himself	* **him**	himself
2.	* **hymn**	hymns	hymnal	hymnal
3.	slim	slims	slimmed	slimming
4.	rim	rims	rimmed	rimming
5.	trim	trims	trimmed	trimming
6.	brim	brims	brimmed	brimming
7.	grim	prim	trimmer	trimmest
8.	dim	dims	dimmed	dimming
9.	**swim**	swims	swam/swum	**swimming**
10.	Tim	Tim's	Timothy	Timothy's
11.	victim	victims	* **Jim**	* **Jim's**
12.	whim	whims	* **gym**	* **gyms**
13.	shim	shims	shimmed	shimming
14.	skim	skims	skimmed	skimming
15.	Kim	Kim's whim	limb	limbs
16.	amp	amps	**camper**	campers
17.	**camp**	camps	camped	camping
18.	**champ**	champs	champion	champions
19.	lamp	lamps	championship	championships
20.	clamp	clamps	clamped	clamping
21.	tamp	tamps	tamped	tamping
22.	**stamp**	**stamps**	stamped	stamping
23.	ramp	ramps	scamp	scamps
24.	tramp	tramps	tramped	tramping
25.	cramp	**cramps**	cramped	cramping

* Homophones:

him/hymn	Please don't let him sing a hymn.
Jim/gym	Jim loves to play in a gym.
Jim's/gyms	He owns and operates several of Jim's gyms.

See the complete -im family on p. 118 in TPES; the -amp, p. 269; the -ion, p. 843.

	85th day	86th day	87th day	88th day
1.	damp	damper	dampers	dampest
2.	dampen	dampens	dampened	dampening
3.	* week	weeks	weekend	weekends
4.	* peek	peeks	peeked	peeking
5.	reek	reeks	reeked	reeking
6.	creek	creeks	* leek	* leeks
7.	cheek	cheeks	sleek	meek
8.	seek	seeks	sought	seeking
9.	shriek	shrieks	shrieked	shrieking
10.	* weak	weaker	weakest	* weakly
11.	weaken	weakens	weakened	weakening
12.	beak	beaks	beaker	beakers
13.	* peak	peaks	sneaker	sneakers
14.	speak	speaks	spoke/spoken	speaking
15.	streak	streaks	streaked	streaking
16.	sneak	sneaks	sneaked	sneaking
17.	* creak	creaks	creaked	creaking
18.	squeak	squeaks	squeaked	squeaking
19.	freak	freaks	freaked	freaking
20.	* leak	leaks	leaked	leaking
21.	teak	speaker	speakers	squeaky
22.	sleep	sleeps	slept	sleeping
23.	oversleep	oversleeps	overslept	oversleeping
24.	asleep	sleeper	sleepers	* clothes
25.	keep	keeps	kept	keeping

* Homophones:

week/weak	All week I felt weak.
peek/peak/pique	A peek at Pike's Peak might pique your curiosity.
creek/creak	Creek rhymes with either seek or sick. Creak rhymes with reek.
weekly/weakly	The weekly paper is very weakly supported.
leek/leak	A leek is vegetable. A leak can sink a ship.
clothes/close	They had to close the used clothes store.

See the complete -amp family on p. 269 in *The Patterns of English Spelling* (TPES); the -eek, p. 408; the -eak, p. 408; the -eep, p. 424.

	89th day	90th day	91st day	92nd day
1.	weep	weeps	**wept**	weeping
2.	**sweep**	sweeps	**swept**	sweeping
3.	creep	creeps	**crept**	creeping
4.	peep	peeps	peeped	peeping
5.	seep	seeps	seeped	seeping
6.	steep	steeps	steeped	steeping
7.	**sheep**	**jeep**	jeeps	*** clothes**
8.	deep	deeper	deepest	deeply
9.	beep	beeps	beeped	beeping
10.	*** cheep**	cheeps	cheeped	cheeping
11.	*** cheap**	cheaper	cheapest	cheaply
12.	leap	leaps	leaped	leaping
13.	heap	heaps	heaped	heaping
14.	reap	reaps	reaped	reaping
15.	steeple	steeples	**aren't**	**doesn't**
16.	**people**	people's choice	**people**	people's voice
17.	pep	peps	pepped	pepping
18.	pepper	peppers	peppered	peppering
19.	step	steps	stepped	stepping
20.	misstep	missteps	instep	footsteps
21.	Abe	Abe's name	Abraham	Abraham's nickname
22.	babe	babes	Babe Ruth	Babe Ruth's bat
23.	**baby**	**babies**	**babied**	**babying**
24.	**able**	unable	**ability**	disability
25.	disable	disables	disabled	disabling

* Homophones:

cheap/cheep   What do you call an inexpensive bird call? A cheap cheep.
close/clothes   We bought some new clothes at the close out sale.

See the complete -eep family on p. 424 in *The Patterns of English Spelling* (TPES);
the -eap, p. 424; the -ep, p. 127; the -abe, p. 320; -able, p. 610; -ple, 612.

	93rd day	94th day	95th day	96th day
1.	enable	enables	enabled	enabling
2.	table	tables	tabled	tabling
3.	stable	stables	stability	inability
4.	cable	cables	cabled	cabling
5.	fable	fables	fabled	abilities
6.	gable	gables	gabled	disabilities
7.	sable	* we're	* were	* (Am.) color
8.	Bible	Bibles	I'd	I've
9.	noble	nobles	nobility	* (Br.) colour
10.	ruble	rubles	* we're	* aunts
11.	feeble	feebler	feeblest	many
12.	* made	shadow	shadows	shadowed
13.	shade	shades	shaded	shading
14.	* wade	wades	waded	wading
15.	fade	fades	faded	fading
16.	blade	blades	glade	glades
17.	trade	trades	traded	trading
18.	jade	jaded	trader	traders
19.	crusade	crusades	crusaded	crusading
20.	* spade	spades	crusader	crusaders
21.	persuade	persuades	persuaded	persuading
22.	lemonade	persuader	persuaders	persuasion
23.	invade	invaded	invading	invasion
24.	evade	evading	evaded	evasion
25.	abrade	abrades	abrasive	abrasion

* Homophones:

we're/were	We're going to go there. Were you ever there?
made/maid	Who made the bed? The maid.
wade/weighed	I like to wade into the water. He weighed a ton.
spade/spayed	You can dig with a spade. A dog may be spayed.
color/colour	In the United States, Americans color. In Great Britain, the British colour.
aunts/ants/aunt's	I have aunts and uncles. My aunt's pet ants were poisoned.

NOTE: Because we read writers who use American spellings and writers who use British spellings, AVKO chooses to present both. As a teacher you are free to choose whichever you feel is most appropriate for your children. Teach either or both. It's your choice.

See the complete -ble family on p. 610 in TPES; the -ade, p. 321.

44

	97th day	98th day	99th day	100th day
1.	* **mail**	mails	mailed	mailing
2.	nail	nails	nailed	nailing
3.	snail	snails	sailor	sailors
4.	* **sail**	sails	sailed	sailing
5.	* **bail**	bails	bailed	bailing
6.	fail	fails	failed	failing
7.	* **Gail**	Gail's	failure	failures
8.	* **hail**	hails	hailed	hailing
9.	blackmail	blackmails	blackmailed	blackmailing
10.	* **pail**	pails	railroad	railroads
11.	rail	rails	railed	railing
12.	trail	trails	trailed	trailing
13.	* **male**	males	trailer	trailers
14.	female	females	**because**	my **aunt's** cat
15.	* **bale**	bales	baled	baling
16.	* **gale**	gales	(Am.) **color**	(Am.) **coloring**
17.	regale	regales	regaled	regaling
18.	* **hale**	been	(Br.) **colour**	(Br.) **colouring**
19.	inhale	inhales	inhaled	inhaling
20.	exhale	exhales	exhaled	exhaling
21.	* **sale**	sales	salesman	salesmen
22.	* **pale**	pales	paled	paling
23.	impale	impales	impaled	impaling
24.	Dale	Dale's	**before**	**before**
25.	scale	scales	scaled	scaling

* Homophones:

male/mail	What do you call letters for men only? Male mail.
sale/sail	What do you call a special on canvas? A sail sale.
bale/bail	You bale hay and cotton. You bail out a boat or post bail.
gale/Gail/Gayle	A gale is a wind storm. Gail's last name is Storm. So is Gayle's.
hale/hail	What do you call hearty ice? Hale hail.
pale/pail	What do you call a sick looking bucket? A pale pail.

See the complete -ale family on p. 422 in (TPES); the -ail, p. 411.

	101st day	102nd day	103rd day	104th day
1.	derail	derails	derailed	derailing
2.	* tail	tails	before	* eye
3.	detail	details	detailed	detailing
4.	retail	retailer	retailers	* clothes
5.	cocktail	cocktails	quail	quails
6.	* wail	wails	wailed	wailing
7.	* whale	whales	whaler	whalers
8.	shale	stale	* tale	tales
9.	* wholesale	wholesaler	wholesalers	tattletale
10.	* ale	ginger ale	ailment	ailments
11.	* ail	ails	ailed	ailing
12.	Al	Al's pals	Allen	Alvin
13.	Hal	Hal's pals	Albert	Sal
14.	pal	Cal	Calvin	Sally
15.	* rain	rains	rained	raining
16.	brain	brains	harebrained	rainy
17.	train	trains	trained	training
18.	grain	grains	trainer	trainers
19.	strain	strains	strained	straining
20.	* plain	plains	strainer	strainers
21.	restrain	restrains	restrained	restraining
22.	* lain	slain	restraint	restraints
23.	sprain	sprains	sprains	sprained
24.	gain	gains	gained	gaining
25.	drain	drains	drained	draining

* Homophones:

tail/tale	What do you call a story about a tail? A tail tale.
wail/whale	What do you call a cry by Moby Dick? A whale wail.
ail/ale	Ail means sick. Ale is a beverage.
lain/lane	Lie, lay, lain. A lane can be a path, street, or alley.
wholesale/hole sale	They had a doughnut hole sale at the wholesale bakery.
rain/rein/reign	During his reign, King Arthur had to rein in his knights when the rain came.
plain/plane	What's an ordinary aircraft? A plain plane.
I/eye/aye	I said "Aye, sir" not "eye sore"!
clothes/close	Please close the clothes closet door.

See the complete -ail family on p. 330 (TPES); the -ale, p. 411; the -al, p. 146; the -ain, p. 419.

	105th day	106th day	107th day	108th day
1.	* **pain**	pains	pained	paining
2.	explain	explains	explained	explaining
3.	* **vain**	explanation	explanations	explanatory
4.	complain	complains	complained	complaining
5.	Spain	Spain's plains	complaint	complaints
6.	stain	stains	stained	staining
7.	entertain	entertains	entertained	entertaining
8.	* **main**	mainly	entertainer	entertainment
9.	remain	remains	remained	remaining
10.	remainder	remainders	**can't**	**can't**
11.	* **ant**	ants	planter	planters
12.	plant	plants	planted	planting
13.	implant	implants	implanted	plantation
14.	slant	slants	slanted	slanting
15.	pant	pants	panted	panting
16.	rant	rants	ranted	ranting
17.	grant	grants	granted	granting
18.	chant	* **chants**	chanted	chanting
19.	enchant	enchants	enchanted	enchanting
20.	*** **want**	**wants**	**wanted**	**wanting**
21.	wad	wads	wadded	wadding
22.	quad	quads	squad	squads
23.	wand	wands	* **break**	**father**
24.	wander	wanders	wandered	wandering
25.	squander	squanders	squandered	squandering

> *** **Note:** See the wa- controlled words on p. 504 of *The Patterns of English Spelling*.

* Homophones:

pane/pain	What do you call it when a window hurts? A pane pain.
vane/vain/vein	A weather vane. A vain person. A vein of gold (or a blood vessel).
mane/main/Maine	The hair on the back of a horse's neck is a mane. Maine is in New England.
	What is the difference between a main mane and a Maine mane?
	Who is the main man in Maine? Maine's governor.
ant/aunt	What do you call the wife of an ant's uncle? An ant aunt.
chants/chance	What do you call accidental songs? Chance chants.
break/brake	Give me a break. Take your foot off the brake.

See the complete -ain family on p. 419 in *The Patterns of English Spelling* (TPES); the -ant, p. 249.

	109th day	110th day	111th day	112th day
1.	**went**	pent	**spent**	penthouse
2.	vent	vents	vented	venting
3.	ventilate	ventilates	ventilated	ventilation
4.	event	events	eventual	eventually
5.	invent	invents	invented	inventing
6.	inventor	inventors	invention	inventions
7.	prevent	prevents	prevented	preventing
8.	* **cent**	* **cents**	prevention	preventative
9.	* **scent**	* **scents**	scented	scenting
10.	* **sent**	* **we're**	(Am.) colored	**doesn't**
11.	* **assent**	assents	assented	assenting
12.	* **dissent**	dissents	dissented	dissenting
13.	dissention	dissident	dissidents	* **aunts**
14.	* **ascent**	ascents	ascension	**been**
15.	* **descent**	descents	(Br.) coloured	**before**
16.	decent	decently	decency	decent
17.	absent	**where**	**where**	**where**
18.	**tent**	* **tents**	break-in	**fathers**
19.	intent	* **intents**	intentions	intentional
20.	Be con**tent**.He con**tents** himself.		We are con**tent**ed.	contentment
21.	the **con**tent of	the **con**tents	eyeball	eyeful
22.	cement	cements	cemented	cementing
23.	We **lent** him $2.00.	Lenten	demented	**aren't**
24.	extent	extension	renter	renters
25.	**rent**	rents	rented	renting

---

* Homophones:

cent/scent/sent	What's a penny mailed? A sent cent. A cheap smell? A one cent scent.
cents/scents/sense	What's penny smarts? Cents sense. Smelling smarts? Scents sense.
assent/ascent	What's an agreement to go up? Ascent assent.
dissent/descent	What's a disagreement about going down? Descent dissent.
intense/intents/in tents	What are strong purposes inside Arab dwellings? Intense intents in tents.
tents/tense	What are uptight Arab dwellings? Tense tents.

NOTE: The author once thought the phrase, "For all **intents and** purposes" was "For all **intensive** purposes!" Ugh! Phrases such as "for all **intents** and purposes" that are heard more often than read can make for unusual misspellings that computers can't catch.

See the complete -ent family on p. 250 in *The Patterns of English Spelling* (TPES).

48

	113th day	114th day	115th day	116th day
1.	pint	pints	half pint	half pints
2.	print	* prints	printed	printing
3.	imprint	imprints	imprinted	imprinting
4.	misprint	misprints	misprinted	misprinting
5.	reprint	reprints	reprinted	reprinting
6.	hint	hints	hinted	hinting
7.	flint	flints	lint	winter
8.	glint	glints	glinted	glinting
9.	splint	splints	splinter	splinters
10.	sprint	sprints	sprinted	sprinting
11.	quint	* quints	sprinter	sprinters
12.	squint	squints	squinted	squinting
13.	tint	tints	tinted	tinting
14.	stint	stints	printer	printers
15.	mint	* mints	minted	minting
16.	green	greens	greener	greenest
17.	screen	screens	screened	screening
18.	wintergreen	* seen	sheen	keen
19.	colleen	colleens	teen	teens
20.	queen	queens	thirteen	fourteen
21.	between	in between	canteen	canteens
22.	Halloween	foreseen	fifteen	sixteen
23.	* lean	leans	leaned	leaning
24.	clean	cleans	cleaned	cleaning
25.	* mean	means	meant	meaning

* Homophones:

prince/prints	What does a king's son do when he writes? The prince prints.
quince/quints	What fruit is named after quintuplets. The quints' quince.
mince/mints	What means to chop up candies? Mince mints.
mean/mien	What do you call a bad attitude? A mean mien.
lean/lien	Bankers will lean toward attaching a lien on your property.
scene/seen	Have you seen the latest scene?

See the complete -int family on p. 251 in *The Patterns of English Spelling* (TPES);
the -een, p. 420; the -ean, p. 420.

	117th day	118th day	119th day	120th day
1.	**mean**	meaner	meanest	meanly
2.	* **bean**	**beans**	beaned	beaning
3.	* **Jean**	**Jean's jeans**	dean	deans
4.	glean	gleans	gleaned	gleaning
5.	gleaner	gleaners	cleaners	cleanest
6.	wean	weans	weaned	weaning
7.	**have * been**	**has been**	**who'd**	**coming**
8.	**fine**	fines	* **fined**	fining
9.	define	defines	defined	defining
10.	nine	nines	definition	definitions
11.	canine	canines	definite	**definitely**
12.	refine	refines	refined	refining
13.	**pine**	pines	refinery	refinement
14.	confine	confines	confined	confining
15.	porcupine	porcupines	confinement	**dinner** in a diner
16.	**dine**	dines	dined	**dining room**
17.	**mine**	mines	* **mined**	mining
18.	undermine	undermined	* **miner**	undermining
19.	spine	spines	spinal	**clothes**
20.	vine	vines	final	**finally**
21.	divine	divinely	divinity	**hasn't**
22.	twine	twines	twined	twining
23.	**shine**	shines	shined/shone	**shining**
24.	sunshine	moonshine	swine	**haven't**
25.	* **whine**	whines	whined	whining

* Homophones:

been/bean	Depending on dialect spoken. My bean may have been broken.
been/bin	Depending on dialect spoken. My tool bin may have been messed up.
been/Ben	Depending on dialect spoken. Ben may have been there.
miner/minor	What is a young digger? A minor miner.
wine/whine	What is a cry for more of the grape? A wine whine.
Jean/Gene/gene	Jean wears blue jeans. Gene's genes were inherited.
fined/find	You may be fined if you find fault with the judge.
mined/mind	I hope you don't mind that I once mined for gold.

** Heteronyms:

Jean/Jean — In English names, Jean rhymes with dean. In names from the French, like Jean Paul Trudeau, Jean ("ZHAWN") rhymes with lawn.

See the complete -ean family on p. 420 and the -ine on p. 337 in *The Patterns of English Spelling*.

Evaluation Test #3
(After 120 Days)

		Pattern being tested	Lesson word is in
1.	Do you know if their plane has arr**ived** yet?	ived	75
2.	Harry had a little l**amb** chop.	amb	77
3.	Our spelling should constantly be impr**oving**.	oving	80
4.	The gardener just tr**immed** the hedges.	immed	83
5.	We went tr**amping** through the countryside.	amping	84
6.	Did you get a new pair of sn**eakers**?	eakers	88
7.	Let a sl**eeping** dog lie.	eeping	88
8.	We just st**epped** over the little water puddle.	epped	91
9.	We gave him a h**eaping** helping of oatmeal.	eaping	92
10.	We sh**aded** our eyes from the blazing sun.	aded	95
11.	They were always tr**ading** baseball cards.	ading	96
12.	Have you ever been camping in a tr**ailer**?	ailer	99
13.	Inh**aling** second-hand smoke is bad for your health.	aling	100
14.	The team's tr**ainer** was held in high respect.	ainer	103
15.	I hate it when my sinuses are dr**aining**.	aining	104
16.	Have you ever seen an ench**anted** castle?	anted	107
17.	Our dog keeps w**andering** all around town.	andering	108
18.	Edison inv**ented** a lot of different things.	ented	111
19.	An ounce of prev**ention** is worth a pound of cure.	ention	111
20.	I hate getting spl**inters** in my fingers.	inters	116

Name_____ Date_____

Test #3

1. Do you know if their plane has arr_____ yet?

2. Harry had a little l_____ chop.

3. Our spelling should constantly be impr_____.

4. The gardener just tr_____ the hedges.

5. We went tr_____ through the countryside.

6. Did you get a new pair of sn_____?

7. Let a sl_____ dog lie.

8. We just st_____ over the little water puddle.

9. We gave him a h_____ helping of oatmeal.

10. We sh_____ our eyes from the blazing sun.

11. They were always tr_____ baseball cards.

12. Have you ever been camping in a tr_____?

13. Inh_____ second-hand smoke is bad for your health.

14. The team's tr_____ was held in high respect.

15. I hate it when my sinuses are dr_____.

16. Have you ever seen an ench_____ castle?

17. Our dog keeps w_____ all around town.

18. Edison inv_____ a lot of different things.

19. An ounce of prev_____ is worth a pound of cure.

20. I hate getting spl_____ in my fingers.

	121st day	122nd day	123rd day	124th day
1.	outshine	outshines	outshined/outshone	outshining
2.	**dine**	diners	**been**	**before**
3.	brine	**dinners**	**father's**	**isn't**
4.	shrine	shrines	father-in-law	*** It's too cold.**
5.	combine	combines	combined	combining
6.	tine	tines	turpentine	combination
7.	**line**	lines	lined	**lining**
8.	underline	underlines	underlined	underlining
9.	Mr. Cline	liner	liners	recliner
10.	decline	declines	declined	declining
11.	incline	inclines	inclined	inclining
12.	equine	feline	bovine	inclination
13.	staff	staffs	staffed	staffing
14.	gaff	gaffs	gaffed	gaffing
15.	**laugh**	**laughs**	**laughed**	laughing
16.	Jeff	Jeff's	Mr. Neff	**laughter**
17.	**of**	**haven't**	**four**	fours
18.	**off**	*** break**	break-in	**fourth**
19.	scoff	scoffs	scoffed	scoffing
20.	doff	doffs	doffed	doffing
21.	aft	**after**	rafter	rafters
22.	raft	rafts	rafted	rafting
23.	graft	grafts	grafted	grafting
24.	craft	crafts	crafted	a crafty person
25.	shaft	shafts	shafted	shafting

* Homophones:

it's/its	It's too bad your dog hurt its leg.
rine/Rhine	A good German would never throw a watermelon rine into the Rhine River.
break/brake	It's no fun to break an arm. He stepped on the brake.

See the complete -ine family on p. 337 in *The Patterns of English Spelling* (TPES);
the -aff, p. 141; the -eff, p. 142; the -off, p. 144; -aft, p. 232.

	125th day	126th day	127th day	128th day
1.	* **draft**	drafts	drafted	drafting
2.	* **draught**	draughts	draughted	draughting
3.	**left**	lefts	heft	hefty
4.	theft	thefts	bereft	heftier
5.	**eat**	**eats**	**ate/eaten**	**eating**
6.	* **beat**	**beats**	**beat/beaten**	**beating**
7.	* **feat**	**feats**	**who'd**	**aunt's**
8.	defeat	defeats	defeated	defeating
9.	**meat**	meats	fatherly	**It's too hot.**
10.	**peat**	who're	* **heart**	**heart**
11.	repeat	repeats	repeated	repeating
12.	neat	wheat	repetitive	repetition
13.	fatherhood	* **fourth**	repetition	repetitive
14.	seat	seats	seated	seating
15.	cheat	cheats	cheated	cheating
16.	bleat	bleats	bleated	bleating
17.	pleat	pleats	pleated	pleating
18.	cleat	cleats	**treatment**	treatments
19.	treat	treats	treated	treating
20.	retreat	retreats	retreated	retreating
21.	**heat**	heats	heated	**heating**
22.	* **great**	* **greater**	**greatest**	heaters
23.	**sweat**	sweats	sweating	**sweaters**
24.	**threat**	threats	threat	threats
25.	**threaten**	threatens	**threatened**	threatening

* Homophones:

draft/draught	In the U.S., we draft soldiers, drink draft beer, and write drafts.
	In England, they conscript soldiers, drink draught beer, and write draughts.
beat/beet	You can beat a drum. You can beat an egg. You can eat a beet.
feat/feet	Touching your nose with your toes is a feet feat.
fourth/forth/4th	Going forth is not coming in fourth or even 4th.
great/grate	It's great to charbroil a steak over a grate.
greater/grater	What do you need for better grated cheese? A greater grater.
heart/hart	He didn't have the heart to kill the hart (deer).

See the complete -aft family on p. 232 in *The Patterns of English Spelling* (TPES);
the -eft, p. 232; the -eat, p. 427.

	129th day	130th day	131st day	132nd day
1.	**date**	dates	dated	**dating**
2.	* **gate**	gates	**It's too** bad.	It hurt **its** paw.
3.	irrigate	irrigates	irrigating	irrigation
4.	irritate	irritates	irritating	irritation
5.	skate	skates	skated	**skating**
6.	**late**	**lately**	**later**	**latest**
7.	relate	related	relating	relation
8.	plate	plates	plated	relationship
9.	slate	slates	slated	relatives
10.	mate	mates	mated	mating
11.	cremate	cremated	cremating	cremation
12.	create	created	creating	creation
13.	* **grate**	* **grates**	grateful	gratefully
14.	* **great**	* **greats**	gratitude	ungrateful
15.	**hate**	hates	hating	hateful
16.	**state**	states	statement	station
17.	reinstate	reinstates	reinstatement	reinstating
18.	probate	probates	probating	probation
19.	vacate	vacated	vacating	**vacation**
20.	indicate	indicated	indicating	indication
21.	dedicate	dedicated	dedicating	dedication
22.	**locate**	located	locating	**location**
23.	**educate**	educated	educator	**education**
24.	validate	validated	validating	validation
25.	consolidate	consolidated	consolidating	consolidation

*Homophones:

gate/gait   If a gate could run, it would have a gate gait.
grate/great   What's the best thing to cook a steak on? A great grate.
grates/greats   Talking about military greats grates on my nerves.

See the complete -ate/-ation family on pages 347-353 in *The Patterns of English Spelling*.

	133rd day	134th day	135th day	136th day
1.	**timid**	timidity	timid	**timid**
2.	in**timid**ate	intimidated	intimidating	in**timid**ation
3.	accommodate	accommodated	accommodating	accommodations
4.	segregate	segregated	segregating	segregating
5.	congregate	congregated	congregating	congregating
6.	congress	congressman	congressmen	congressional
7.	obligate	obligates	obligating	obligation
8.	investigate	investigates	investigating	investigation
9.	appreciate	appreciates	appreciated	appreciation
10.	** **associate**	associated	associating	association
11.	radiate	radiated	radiating	radiation
12.	violate	violating	violator	violation
13.	isolate	isolated	isolating	isolation
14.	translate	translated	translator	translation
15.	calculate	calculated	calculator	calculation
16.	regulate	regulated	regular	regulation
17.	insulate	insulated	insulating	insulation
18.	congratulate	congratulated	congratulating	congratulations
19.	fascinate	fascinates	fascinating	fascination
20.	eliminate	eliminates	eliminating	elimination
21.	crime	crimes	criminal	criminals
22.	incriminate	incriminates	incriminating	incrimination
23.	discriminate	discriminates	discriminating	discrimination
24.	dominate	dominates	dominating	domination
25.	nominate	nominates	nominated	nomination

** Heteronyms:

associate ("uh SOH see AY't")   I associate with him.
associate ("uh SOH see it")   He is my associate.
                                 I associate with my associates.
                                 He associates with his associates.

See the complete -ate/ation family on pages 347-353; the -ate ("it") family on pages 354-355 in *The Patterns of English Spelling*.

	137th day	138th day	139th day	140th day
1.	donate	donated	donating	donations
2.	hibernate	hibernates	hibernating	hibernation
3.	take part	particle	particles	**clothes**
4.	participate	participates	participating	participation
5.	anticipate	anticipates	anticipating	anticipation
6.	** **separate**	separates	separated	separation
7.	** **separate** rooms	separately	separatism	separately
8.	celebrate	celebrates	celebrating	celebration
9.	vibrate	vibrates	vibrating	vibration
10.	liberate	liberates	liberating	liberation
11.	** to **deliberate**	deliberates	deliberating	deliberation
12.	** **deliberate**	deliberately	deliberate	deliberately
13.	**considerate**	considerately	considerate	considerately
14.	exaggerate	exaggerates	exaggerating	exaggeration
15.	refrigerate	refrigerator	refrigerators	refrigeration
16.	tolerate	tolerated	tolerant	toleration
17.	**operate**	operator	operators	operation
18.	cooperate	cooperates	cooperating	cooperation
19.	integrate	integrated	integrating	integration
20.	disintegrate	disintegrates	disintegrating	disintegration
21.	migrate	migrant	migratory	migration
22.	immigrate	immigrant	immigrating	immigration
23.	decorate	decorated	decorator	decoration
24.	vapor	vapors	evaporated	vaporize
25.	evaporate	evaporates	evaporating	evaporation

** **Heteronyms:**

separate ("SEP uh RAY't")   We should separate those two.
separate ("SEP rit")   We should put them in separate rooms.

deliberate ("duh LIB ur RAY't")   The jury needed more time to deliberate.
deliberate ("duh LIB ur rit")   It was no accident. It was a deliberate attempt to kill those weeds.

See the complete -ate/ation family on pages 347-353; the -ate ("it") family on pages 354-355 in *The Patterns of English Spelling.*

	141st day	142nd day	143rd day	144th day
1.	penetrate	penetrated	penetrating	penetration
2.	perpetrate	"perp" is slang	perpetrator	perpetration
3.	arbitrate	arbitrating	arbitrator	arbitration
4.	**concentrate**	concentrated	concentrating	**concentration**
5.	demonstrate	demonstrated	demonstrators	demonstration
6.	illustrate	illustrated	illustrating	illustration
7.	frustrate	frustrated	frustrating	**frustration**
8.	dictate	dictated	dictator	dictation
9.	**imitate**	imitated	imitating	**imitation**
10.	**irritate**	irritated	irritating	irritation
11.	**hesitate**	hesitated	hesitating	**hesitation**
12.	rotate	rotated	rotating	rotation
13.	amputate	amputated	amputating	amputation
14.	** **graduate**	graduated	graduating	**graduation**
15. a	** **graduate** of	two graduates of	gradual	gradually
16.	evacuate	evacuated	evacuating	evacuation
17.	value	values	valued	valuing
18.	evaluate	evaluated	evaluating	evaluation
19.	insinuate	insinuated	insinuating	insinuation
20.	accentuate	accentuated	accentuating	accentuation
21.	punctuate	punctuated	punctuating	punctuation
22.	situate	situated	situating	**situation**
23.	equate	equating	equator	equation
24.	aggravate	aggravated	aggravating	aggravation
25.	elevate	elevated	elevator	elevation

** Heteronyms:

graduate ("GRAD joo AY't")   When are you going to graduate?
graduate ("GRAD joo it")   My brother is a graduate of Michigan State University.

See the complete -ate/ation family on pages 347-353; the -ate ("it") family on pages 354-355 in *The Patterns of English Spelling*.

58

	145th day	146th day	147th day	148th day
1.	**act**	**active**	**actor**	**action**
2.	activate	activated	activating	activation
3.	culture	cultures	agriculture	difficult
4.	cultivate	cultivated	cultivator	cultivation
5.	captive	captives	capture	captured
6.	captivate	captivated	captivating	captivation
7.	motive	motives	("moh TEEF") motif	motifs
8.	motivate	motivates	motivating	motivation
9.	**note**	notes	noted	noting
10.	footnote	footnotes	notable	notation
11.	denote	denotes	denoting	denotation
12.	connote	connotes	connoting	connotation
13.	quote	quotes	quoting	quotation
14.	misquote	misquoted	misquoting	misquotation
15.	**vote**	votes	voted	**voting**
16.	devote	devoted	devoting	devotion
17.	* **mote**	motes	motor	motion
18.	demote	demotes	demoted	demotion
19.	promote	promotes	promoted	promotion
20.	by * **rote**	He * **wrote** it.	He rewrote it.	writing
21.	**dote**	dotes	doted	doting
22.	antidote	antidotes	**tote**	totes
23.	anecdote	anecdotes	**total**	**totally**
24.	**private**	privates	privately	privacy
25.	delicate	delicates	delicately	delicately

* Homophones:

rote/wrote   He wrote what he had memorized or what he had learned by rote.
mote/moat   A speck of dust is a mote. Never go swimming in a moat.

See the complete -ate/ation family on pages 347-353; the -ate ("it") family on pages 354-355; the -ote/otion family on page 358 in *The Patterns of English Spelling*.

149th day	150th day	151st day	152nd day
1. media	media	media	media
2. immediate	immediately	immediate	**immediately**
3. my ** **associate**	my associates	**aren't**	**because**
4. I ** **associate**	He associates	We're associating	association
5. A ** **duplicate** key	Two duplicates	duplicated	* **It's all right**.
6. To ** **duplicate**	He duplicates	duplicating	duplication
7. candid	candidly	Candid Camera	candidly
8. candidate	candidates	candidacy	candidacy
9. a ** **delegate**	many delegates	breaking	**quietly**
10. I will ** **delegate**	He delegates	delegating	delegation
11. very ** **appropriate**	appropriately	appropriate	appropriately
12. We ** **appropriate**	appropriated	appropriation	appropriation
13. chocolate	chocolates	**chocolate**	chocolates
14. climate	climates	climate	climates
15. obstinate	obstinately	obstinate	obstinately
16. **fortune**	fortunes	* **you'll**	* **one**
17. **fortunate**	fortunately	* **you're**	* **one-half**
18. unfortunate	unfortunately	* **heart**	hearty
19. pirate	pirates	pirating	piracy
20. literate	literal	literally	literacy
21. illiterate	illiterates	literature	illiteracy
22. ** **deliberate**	deliberately	** **deliberate**	deliberately
23. We deliberated	he deliberates	deliberating	deliberation
24. **accurate**	accurately	accuracy	inaccurate
25. adequate	adequately	adequacy	inadequate

* Homophones:

you'll/Yule/Ewell/Yul	You'll love the way Ewell and Yul sing Yuletide carols.
you're/your	You're going to love your test results.
one-half/won half	One-half of the contestants won half the two-man races.
It's all right/its awl wright	It's all right to call a town's maker of awls "its awl wright."

** Heteronyms:

associate ("uh SOH see it") / associate ("uh SOH see AY't") My associate will not associate with me.
duplicate ("DOO pluh kit") / duplicate ("DOO pluh KAY't") In duplicate bridge you duplicate the hands.
appropriate ("uh PROH pree it") / appropriate ("uh PROH pree AY't") It's not appropriate to appropriate my property.
delegate ("DEL uh git") / delegate ("DEL uh GAY't") That delegate should delegate some of his work.
deliberate ("duh LIB ur it") / deliberate ("duh LIB ur AY't") Be more deliberate when you deliberate.

See the complete -ate/ation family on pages 347-353; the -ate ("it") family on pages 354-355 in *The Patterns of English Spelling*.

	153rd day	154th day	155th day	156th day
1.	**age**	ages	aged	aging
2.	page	**pages**	paged	paging
3.	rampage	rampages	rampaged	rampaging
4.	cage	cages	caged	caging
5.	**rage**	rages	raged	raging
6.	enrage	enrages	enraged	enraging
7.	* **gauge**	gauges	gauged	gauging
8.	* **gage**	gages	gaged	gaging
9.	engage	engages	**engaged**	engagement
10.	disengage	disengaged	disengaging	disengagement
11.	sage	sages	crag	crags
12.	**stage**	stages	staged	staging
13.	**rag**	rags	ragged	ragging
14.	**bag**	bags	bagged	bagging
15.	**brag**	brags	**bragged**	**bragging**
16.	lag	lags	lagged	lagging
17.	**flag**	flags	flagged	flagging
18.	gag	gags	gagged	gagging
19.	nag	nags	**nagged**	**nagging**
20.	snag	snags	snagged	snagging
21.	sag	sags	sagged	sagging
22.	**tag**	tags	**tagged**	tagging
23.	wag	wags	**wagged**	**wagging**
24.	**drag**	drags	dragged	dragging
25.	zigzag	zigzags	zigzagged	zigzagging

* Homophones:

gauge/gage   To gauge something is to measure it. A gage is something like a glove that
                  the knights of old threw down on the ground as a challenge to combat.

See the complete -age family on p. 327 in *The Patterns of English Spelling* (TPES);
the -ag, p. 111.

	157th day	158th day	159th day	160th day
1.	**bell**	bells	belled	belling
2.	dumbbell	dumbells	**fell**	**hello**
3.	jell	jells	jelly	Jell-o
4.	* **sell**	sells	sold	selling
5.	**tell**	tells	* **told**	**telling**
6.	foretell	foretells	foretold	foretelling
7.	**well**	wells	* **welled**	welling
8.	swell	swells	swelled	swelling
9.	dwell	dwells	dwelled	dwelling
10.	quell	quells	quelled	quelling
11.	smell	smells	smelled	smelling
12.	**spell**	spells	spelled	spelling
13.	misspell	misspells	**misspelled**	misspelling
14.	**shell**	shells	shelled	shelling
15.	* **cell**	cells	cellular	cellmate
16.	dell	dells	pell-mell	Nell
17.	**yell**	yells	yelled	yelling
18.	**yellow**	yellows	yellowed	yellowing
19.	bellow	bellows	bellowed	bellowing
20.	mellow	mellows	mellowed	mellowing
21.	**fellow**	fellows	swollen	droll
22.	* **roll**	rolls	rolled	rolling
23.	troll	trolls	trolled	trolling
24.	toll	tolls	* **tolled**	tolling
25.	stroll	strolls	strolled	strolling

* Homophones:

told/tolled	The poet told me that the bell tolled for all of us.
weld/welled	My son knows how to weld. Tears welled up in my eyes.
roll/role	What do you call a part in a play for a Danish? A roll role.
sell/cell	A salesman should know how to sell. A prison inmate lives in a cell.

See the complete -ell family on p. 149 in *The Patterns of English Spelling* (TPES); the -oll, p. 153.

Evaluation Test #4
(After 160 Days)

		Pattern Being Tested	Lesson word is in
1.	Her new suit is at the cl**eaners**.	eaners	119
2.	I can't stand people who are always wh**ining**.	ining	120
3.	I'd like to float down the Mississippi on a r**aft**.	aft	121
4.	I think I'd do it just for l**aughs**.	aughs	122
5.	I like to be tr**eated** with some respect. Don't you?	eated	127
6.	They bought each other matching sw**eaters**.	eaters	128
7.	Not everybody loves to go ice sk**ating**.	ating	132
8.	We didn't go anywhere on vac**ation**.	ation	132
9.	Our house needs some new insul**ation**.	ation	136
10.	He went to the hospital for an oper**ation**.	ation	140
11.	Do you understand the situ**ation** that you're in?	ation	144
12.	Husbands should be dev**oted** to their wives.	oted	146
13.	I hope she gets the prom**otion**.	otion	148
14.	Almost everybody loves chocol**ate**.	ate	149
15.	Unfortun**ately**, some people can't eat sweets.	ately	150
16.	The liter**acy** movement is gaining ground.	acy	152
17.	The couple got eng**aged** on St. Valentine's Day.	aged	155
18.	Nobody likes people who are always br**agging**.	agging	156
19.	Nobody likes to missp**ell** a word.	ell	157
20.	The injured elephant b**ellowed** long and loud.	ellowed	159

Name_____ Date_____

Test #4

1. Her new suit is at the cl_____.

2. I can't stand people who are always wh_____.

3. I'd like to float down the Mississippi on a r_____.

4. I think I'd do it just for l_____.

5. I like to be tr_____ with some respect. Don't you?

6. They bought each other matching sw_____.

7. Not everybody loves to go ice sk_____.

8. We didn't go anywhere on vac_____.

9. Our house needs some new insul_____.

10. He went to the hospital for an oper_____.

11. Do you understand the situ_____ that you're in?

12. Husbands should be dev_____ to their wives.

13. I hope she gets the prom_____.

14. Almost everybody loves chocol_____.

15. Unfortun_____ , some people can't eat sweets.

16. The liter_____ movement is gaining ground.

17. The couple got eng_____ on St. Valentine's Day.

18. Nobody likes people who are always br_____.

19. Nobody likes to missp_____ a word.

20. The injured elephant b_____ long and loud.

	161st day	162nd day	163rd day	164th day
1.	enroll	enrolls	enrolled	enrolling
2.	* **poll**	polls	polled	polling
3.	scroll	scrolls	scrolled	scrolling
4.	* **boll**	bolls	knoll	knolls
5.	enroll	enrolls	enrolled	enrolling
6.	**control**	controls	**controlled**	controlling
7.	decontrol	decontrols	decontrolled	decontrolling
8.	patrol	patrols	patrolled	patrolling
9.	extol	extols	extolled	extolling
10.	doll	dolls	all dolled up	dolly
11.	dolly	dollies	Ms. Lolly	lollipop
12.	loll	lolls	lolled	lolling
13.	moll	molls	Molly	Molly's dollies
14.	**dull**	dulls	dulled	dulling
15.	gull	gulls	seagull	seagulls
16.	hull	hulls	hulled	hulling
17.	cull	culls	culled	culling
18.	lull	lulls	lulled	lulling
19.	lullaby	lullabies	skull	skulls
20.	mull	mulls	mulled	mulling
21.	**pull**	pulls	pulled	pulling
22.	**bull**	bulls	bully	bullies
23.	**full**	fully	pulley	pulleys
24.	**help**	helps	helped	helping
25.	yelp	yelps	yelped	yelping

* Homophones:

boll/bole/bowl   A cotton boll. A bowl of cereal. "Bole" is a scrabble word.
poll/pole   What do you call a Polish questionnaire about poles? A Pole pole poll.

See the complete -oll family on p. 153 in *The Patterns of English Spelling* (TPES);
the -ol, p. 152; the -ull, p. 155; the -elp, p. 246.

165th day	166th day	167th day	168th day
1. helpless	helplessly	helplessness	* your friend
2. helpful	helpfully	unhelpful	unhelpfully
3. bank	banks	banked	banking
4. thank	thanks	thanked	thanking
5. lank	thankful	thankfully	bankers
6. blank	blanks	blanked	blanking
7. clank	clanks	clanked	clanking
8. plank	planks	planked	planking
9. flank	flanks	flanked	flanking
10. rank	ranks	ranked	ranking
11. crank	cranks	cranked	cranking
12. frank	frankly	frankness	frankfurter
13. prank	pranks	prankster	pranksters
14. spank	spanks	spanked	spanking
15. tank	tanks	tanker	tankers
16. yank	yanks	yanked	yanking
17. ankle	ankles	* you're nice	you're quiet
18. rankle	rankles	rankled	rankling
19. ink	inks	inked	inking
20. sink	sinks	sank/sunk	sinking
21. drink	drinks	drank/drunk	drinking
22. shrink	shrinks	shrank/shrunk	shrinking
23. stink	stinks	stank/stunk	stinking
24. link	* links	linked	linking
25. blink	blinks	blinked	blinking

* Homophones:

lynx/links   What do you call a golf course for wildcats? A lynx links.
you're/your   You're going to miss your plane if you don't hurry up.

See the complete -ank family on p. 220 in *The Patterns of English Spelling* (TPES); the -ink, p. 221; the -ankle, p. 605.

	169th day	170th day	171st day	172nd day
1.	slink	slinks	slinked	slinking
2.	**wink**	winks	winked	winking
3.	mink	minks	brink	brinks
4.	chink	chinks	chinked	chinking
5.	**think**	**thinks**	**thought**	**thinking**
6.	kink	kinks	kinked	kinking
7.	**pink**	pinks	**uncle**	**uncles**
8.	zinc	zinc	zinc	zinc
9.	Lincoln	Lincoln's	Lincoln St.	Lincoln Ave.
10.	twinkle	twinkles	twinkled	twinkling
11.	**wrinkle**	wrinkles	**wrinkled**	wrinkling
12.	sprinkle	sprinkles	sprinkled	**sprinkling**
13.	sprinkler	sprinklers	blinker	blinkers
14.	*** web**	webs	webbed feet	webbing
15.	ebb	ebbs	ebbed	ebbing
16.	Mr. *** Webb**	Miss Webb's	Jeb	Jeb's cab
17.	**leg**	**legs**	legging	leggings
18.	**beg**	**begs**	**begged**	**begging**
19.	peg	pegs	pegged	pegging
20.	**egg**	**eggs**	egged	egging
21.	keg	kegs	nutmeg	dregs
22.	honk	honks	honked	honking
23.	conk	conks	conked	conking
24.	donkey	donkeys	**hasn't**	**haven't**
25.	monk	monks	**monkey**	monkeys

---

* Homophones:

web/Webb   A spider web owned by Mr. Webb would be a Webb web.

See the complete -ink family on p. 221 in *The Patterns of English Spelling* (TPES);
the -inkle, p. 605; the -eg, p. 112; the -onk, p. 222.

	173rd day	174th day	175th day	176th day
1.	**trunk**	trunks	drunk	drunks
2.	dunk	dunks	dunked	dunking
3.	bunk	bunks	bunked	bunking
4.	**junk**	junks	junked	junking
5.	plunk	plunks	plunked	plunking
6.	clunk	clunks	clunked	clunking
7.	flunk	flunks	flunked	flunking
8.	**sunk**	gunk	hunk	hunks
9.	chunk	chunks	slunk	*** "thunk"
10.	**skunk**	skunks	**skunked**	skunking
11.	**uncle**	uncles	my **uncle's** car	**Uncle** Jim
12.	bookrack	gun rack	hat rack	hunchback
13.	tailback	swayback	touchback	hogback
14.	playback	cutback	feedback	drawback
15.	airsick	seasick	carsick	homesick
16.	toothpick	candlestick	joystick	lipstick
17.	shipwreck	bottleneck	roughneck	rubberneck
18.	paycheck	foredeck	fore-check	bodycheck
19.	o'clock	peacock	poppycock	deadlock
20.	hemlock	bedrock	livestock	oarlock
21.	roadblock	sunblock	shamrock	gridlock
22.	woodchuck	sawbuck	unstuck	potluck
23.	duckling	darling	starling	dumpling
24.	yearling	bedsprings	upswing	downswing
25.	herring	Wyoming	ringside	ringworm

*** **Note:** The word "thunk" is sometimes used by writers to indicate a dull metallic sound or as a nonstandard past tense of the word think (cf. drink, drank, drunk to think, "thank," "thunk"). When a writer does the latter, it is usually humorous and also indicates the speaker is probably uneducated.

See the complete -unk family on p. 222 in *The Patterns of English Spelling* (TPES); the -ack, p. 214; the -ick, p. 215; the -ock, p. 216; -uck, p. 216; -ing, p. 218.

177th day	178th day	179th day	180th day
1. dedicated	two delegates	navy	radius
2. dedication	delegated	navigate	radial
3. indicating	delegation	navigator	radiate
4. indication	valid	navigation	radiation
5. medic	validate	irrigate	media
6. medicine	validation	irrigation	mediate
7. medicinal	timid	irritate	mediator
8. medical	intimidate	irritating	mediation
9. medicated	intimidation	irritation	immediate
10. medication	commode	investigate	immediately
11. implicate	commodity	investigator	remediate
12. implicated	accommodate	investigating	remedial
13. implications	accommodating	investigations	remediation
14. ** syndicate	accommodations	negotiate	fury
15. syndicated	create	negotiated	furies
16. syndication	creating	negotiating	furious
17. complicated	creation	negotiations	infuriate
18. complications	oblige	appreciate	infuriated
19. communicate	obliged	appreciated	abbreviate
20. communicating	obligated	appreciation	abbreviated
21. communications	obligations	office	abbreviation
22. lubricated	congregate	officer	alleviate
23. lubrication	congregated	official	alleviated
24. educated	congregating	officiate	alleviating
25. education	congregation	officiating	alleviation

** Heteronyms:

syndicate ("SIN duh kit") / syndicate ("sin duh KAY't") A syndicate may syndicate cartoons.

FINAL EVALUATION TEST

		Pattern being tested	Lesson word is in
1.	My neighbor has a lot of neph**ews** and nieces.	ews	2
2.	It finally d**awned** on me that I goofed.	awned	7
3.	My neighbor makes a living t**uning** pianos.	uning	12
4.	I was h**oping** that you would ask that question.	oping	16
5.	I hope everybody is rel**axed** and enjoying this test.	axed	27
6.	We had to get our old t**oaster** repaired.	oaster	32
7.	I wish you would stop h**umming** that song.	umming	44
8.	We scr**ubbed** and waxed the floor.	ubbed	59
9.	They bought a used car inst**ead** of a new one.	ead	63
10.	I know that you all are impr**oving** your spelling.	oving	80
11.	I hope I am not st**epping** on anybody's toes.	epping	92
12.	Does anybody know who inv**ented** television?	ented	111
13.	An ounce of prev**ention** is worth a pound of cure.	ention	111
14.	I have to stop by the cl**eaners** on the way home.	eaners	119
15.	They tr**eated** us as if we were royalty.	eated	127
16.	I think that they are sk**ating** on thin ice.	ating	132
17.	This situ**ation** calls for tact and diplomacy.	ation	144
18.	Did your sister get the prom**otion**?	otion	148
19.	Let others do the br**agging** for you.	agging	156
20.	I'm glad we all contr**olled** our tempers.	olled	163
21.	Very few people are completely h**elp**less.	elp	165
22.	We should all be th**ank**ful.	ank	166
23.	The lawyer had a tw**inkle** in her eye.	inkle	169
24.	The defendant b**egged** the judge for mercy.	egged	171
25.	The car was totaled. So we j**unked** it.	unked	175

Name_____ Date_____

Final Evaluation Test

1. My neighbor has a lot of neph_____ and nieces.

2. It finally d_____ on me that I goofed.

3. My neighbor makes a living t_____ pianos.

4. I was h_____ that you would ask that question.

5. I hope everybody is rel_____ and enjoying this test.

6. We had to get our old t_____ repaired.

7. I wish you would stop h_____ that song.

8. We scr_____ and waxed the floor.

9. They bought a used car inst_____ of a new one.

10. I know that you all are impr_____ your spelling.

11. I hope I am not st_____ on anybody's toes.

12. Does anybody know who inv_____ television?

13. An ounce of prev_____ is worth a pound of cure.

14. I have to stop by the cl_____ on the way home.

15. They tr_____ us as if we were royalty.

16. I think that they are sk_____ on thin ice.

17. This situ_____ calls for tact and diplomacy.

18. Did your sister get the prom_____?

19. Let others do the br_____ for you.

20. I'm glad we all contr_____ our tempers.

21. Very few people are completely h_____less.

22. We should all be th_____ful.

23. The lawyer had a tw_____ in her eye.

24. The defendant b_____ the judge for mercy.

25. The car was totaled. So we j_____ it.